ENDORSEMENT

"As a happily married woman of forty-eight years, I found this book to be very enlightening. Several of my friends and relatives are widowed or divorced, and they are starting the dating scene. . . again. This book helped me become aware of their journey through loss, trials, depression, and finally the success of living again and becoming whole. This book covers many subjects that women of all ages will probably go through at some point in their lives. It is a must read that will help readers understand a woman's journey through life."

J. K. Davis, author, quilter, teacher, and friend.

Learning to Dance in the Rain

Best Wishes
Always

Shelby Wagner
Feb. 4, 2019

LEARNING to Dance in the RAIN

*Dealing with Grief,
Moving On and
Online Dating*

SHELBY WAGNER

XULON **PRESS**

Xulon Press
2301 Lucien Way #415
Maitland, FL 32751
407.339.4217
www.xulonpress.com

Unless otherwise indicated, scripture quotations are taken from The King James Version (KJV) – *public domain*.

Printed in the United States of America.

ISBN-13: 978-1-54565-292-3

TABLE OF CONTENTS

INTRODUCTION

H ave you recently lost your loved one? If so, then you are probably still hurting. Perhaps this book will help. Losing a loved one is a catastrophic event and one of the most difficult events in our lives. At the time this happens to us, we are devastated and our thoughts can spur up questions like, "What if I had done this?' or "I should have done that!" and "How can I live without him or her?"

"Learning to Dance in the Rain" is the story of the author's own struggle to deal with the loss of her husband of fifty years, her journey through the grief-process into acceptance and the building of a completely new life as an independent single adult woman of seventy-five. Along the way several women have commented to Shelby that they admire her bravery and strength, adding that they "could not have done what she has done." Shelby shrugs as she responds, "We do not know what we can do until we are faced with adversity. Then we do what we have to do."

The book concludes with an introduction to the world of Internet Dating with its advantages and disadvantages while advising its readers to guard their hearts and their finances from fakers (scammers) intent on stealing their money. No one will want to miss this!

DEDICATION

T his book is dedicated to my wonderful family, Robin, David, Scot, and Luke. Thank you all for your love and support, and for being there whenever I need you. I love you and pray God will bless all of you as He has blessed me.

ACKNOWLEDGEMENTS

T hank you to all my wonderful friends for your love and support and a very special thank you to the friends who have helped me to realize my life-long goal of becoming a published author by taking the time to proofread my manuscript: Josie Briggs, John Day, June Davis, Ken Kooiman, Janet Hutchins, and Samantha Stone. I thank all of you from the bottom of my heart and I appreciate and love every one of you for your encouragement and loving support. Thank you.

FOREWORD

"Shelby's book is inspiring to all women and men. She took a vast subject and divided its complexities into individual sections. It is relatable, intellectual, and investigative. Wagner starts her book as a broken woman and ends a strong one. Her journey through the toils of online dating is eye opening and will be helpful to everyone out there trying to find "the one."

This book is both a self-help guide and a genius approach to conquering romance scammers. Much like a profiler, she brings the essence of a sleuth examining the mysterious men of the internet. Do they want you for you? Are they preying on you? Are they after your money and nothing more? Shelby takes her readers on a ride they won't soon forget."

Samantha Stone, Events Coordinator/ Volunteer Facilitator/
Activities Coordinator
St Joseph County Commission on Aging August 23, 2018.

Life is not
about
Waiting for the
Storm
to Pass;
It is
about
Learning to
Dance in the
Rain. [1]

By: Vivian Greene

Chapter One

THE CATASTROPHIC EVENT

I n January 2000, my husband, Bob, and I retired and moved to Tennessee where we built our dream home in the country. Bob had designed our circular home to take advantage of the beautiful, panoramic view of the Smoky Mountains, and although local carpenters did the physical labor, we were on site most of the time making sure the work was done to our specifications.

We had looked forward to our retirement and felt we had always been blessed throughout our lives. In October 2006, we learned that Bob had cancer and the ten years following that revelation became very challenging as he battled cancer and the heart disease that followed.

In June 2016, we made our annual motor trip to Michigan to visit our daughter, and while there we decided to visit my failing mother, and my sister and her family in the Upper Peninsula. We enjoyed the visit very much, but on the way south, I noticed my husband had developed a deep cough and suggested that we delay going to Tennessee so he could see a doctor. He refused and insisted he was not ill. He just wanted to get home. As the miles sped by, however, I became more and more concerned about him and I told myself that I would stop at a hospital when we got closer to home. But when we got there, Bob again insisted that he was fine and just wanted to go straight home.

The next day, however, he was very weak and decided that he did need to go see the doctor. I helped him into our car and I drove him to the hospital. As soon as we arrived at the emergency entrance, I jumped out of the car and ran inside to get help. An attendant followed me out with a wheelchair, and when she saw how weak Bob was, she rushed him inside, through registration and immediately into the emergency room. The doctor came immediately, asked a few questions and then ordered X-rays and blood work. We had arrived at the hospital at five o'clock that afternoon and at seven were told that Bob had pneumonia and would be admitted to the hospital as soon as a room became available. At ten he was admitted to the hospital and moved into a room there. By midnight he seemed to be getting better. His fever had gone down and his other vitals had returned to normal. Since I was exhausted, and he was being cared for, I asked him if I could go home and get some sleep. He told me to go home and I did.

At six thirty the next morning, I called the nurses' station to check on him, and when there was no answer, I knew I had to get to the hospital right away. When I arrived, I found him extremely agitated. He declared, "I'm not going to make it out of here alive! Get me something to eat!" So I went to find the nurse.

When I found her, she told me that he could not have any food until the intubation procedure was done because he would vomit it back up. I asked why the procedure was needed and she replied that the medicine was not helping him because it was not getting into his lungs. Bob was agitated and needed to breathe more deeply. This procedure would help him to breathe in the medicine and he could not get better without it.

I returned to Bob's room and was trying to explain to him what the nurse had said when the room suddenly filled with several nurses and two doctors who rushed him out of the room. As I grabbed my things to follow, one of the nurses told me they were taking him to ICU, and I needed to wait fifteen minutes and then I could come be with him there.

I never saw him alive again! I waited and waited. Fifteen minutes came and went as I became more and more concerned. Finally, two nurses came and told me, "He didn't make it." I was stunned and unsure that I had heard them correctly. "What? What do you mean, he didn't make it?" I stammered. They replied that his heart had stopped while they were trying to insert the tube.

"Oh, my God! You must do something!" I cried. "There is nothing we can do," they replied. "He is gone." "No, that cannot be!" I declared. They told me again that his heart was unable to take the intubation procedure. It had stopped as they were inserting the tube and they could not start it again. I had given permission. I had signed the paper. Now he was gone. A horrible feeling of pain cut through me like a knife as I thought, *I killed my husband!*

I was devastated! Bob had been rushed to the hospital several times over the past ten years, and he had always come home with me. How could I think this time would be different? His last words hit me in the face, "I'm not going to make it out of this hospital alive!" Did he know what was going to happen? or was he just frustrated with the hospital experience? I will never know.

He had spoken the truth, and I argued with him right to the end. I concluded that I had killed him! Immediately I began chastising myself:

Why didn't I insist on taking him to the hospital earlier?
Why didn't I call 911?
Why did I agree to the intubation?
How could he go without saying goodbye?
This wasn't supposed to happen!
How could God do this to me?
What on earth do I do now?
How am I going to survive without him?

I was overwhelmed and I prayed, "Dear God, please help me! I don't know what to do. Please let it be a mistake. I need him!"

My pastor and a friend from church had arrived a few minutes before I had gotten the news, and we were all stunned. They consoled me, and led me back to my seat. After a few minutes they offered to call my family and I handed them my cellphone.

The coroner came with a form to fill out. He asked me some questions, and wrote down my answers. I asked him what would happen next and he told me to wait for my son to come from North Carolina and then we could go to the room where his body was. When my son arrived, we waited for a while until a nurse came to take us to see Bob. After spending some time there, I gathered up our things and we went home. I felt numb and I felt cold. It was all so strange, as if I were watching a movie of myself moving around the room, picking up his clothes and shoes, tidying the room. I could not believe I was leaving Bob there all alone, or that he would never be coming home with me again. I felt so empty, cold and distant.

I kept whispering to myself over and over again, "Oh Bob! I am so sorry!" My son finally asked, "Mom, why do keep saying that?"

"Because I killed him!" I replied.

"No, Mom, you did not! You did exactly what he wanted," he responded.

When I got home, I lay down on my bed. I felt numb. I was exhausted physically and mentally, but I could not sleep. Questions kept going around in my head and the tears would not stop. My daughter and her family arrived at midnight, after nine hours of riding in a car, and they were exhausted. We fell into our beds and tried to sleep, and the next morning we went to the funeral home to make the final arrangements together. The next two days are a blur. There was so much to do.

The funeral service was beautiful, and the church was filled with friends and family. I was surprised to see so many people. Several had driven quite a distance on such short notice. Bob would also have been surprised and humbled to see the church full. Somehow, I got through the procession, service, his burial in the church cemetery and the dinner that followed.

When it was all over, our immediate family and several close friends went back to my house and and I collapsed into my recliner and fell asleep. Later that evening, all my worries returned, and I was overwhelmed again.

- I thought I had lost over half of my income;
- I had a large mortgage on our home;
- Our home was in the country with the closest neighbor a mile away;
- I had lots of friends in Tennessee but no family;
- What was I going to do now?

That evening, my daughter offered a solution, "Mom, come back to Michigan with us. You can live with us until you sell your house in Tennessee. That will give you time to grieve and to decide what you want to do with the rest of your life. We will help you pack what you need for the next few months." I was overwhelmed by her generous offer, and after discussing it with my son, we all agreed that this was what I should do.

It was a good decision and I will always be grateful to my daughter and her husband for the opportunity to live with them during this terrible time. They were wonderful to me and I felt welcome and comfortable. A bonus was that I had the opportunity to watch as my only grandchild grew from a two-year-old baby boy into a four-year-old small adult.

It was a very sad time and the tears would not stop. I cried until I thought I could not cry any more and then I would start all over again. I did not feel like doing anything, but I forced myself to keep busy. I went to the mall to walk around, I played the piano, I went out to eat and found it very difficult to eat alone. I was sad, lonely and depressed.

Chapter Two

GRIEVING IS NECESSARY

L osing a loved one is catastrophic. It is one of the most painful events which we will ever experience. How does one deal with it? How often do we hear of a surviving spouse who dies within a few weeks or months after his or her partner? Were they lonely? Were they depressed? I am sure they were. How could they not have been? Perhaps they became so overwhelmed with grief and loneliness that they just gave up. At first it is a battle simply to survive alone. I know that during this sad and lonely time I sometimes wished that I had been "taken" also.

What is grief? According to Merriam-Webster.com, it is a "deep and poignant distress caused by or as if in bereavement." [1] Some synonyms are sorrow, anguish and regret. Do those words describe your feelings at this time? They describe mine. I was sad and at times I still am! Sometimes my eyes water and tears gently roll down my cheeks, and sometimes they come suddenly hitting me like a tsunami. A thought will spark a memory and the tears come.

Another memory will come and I smile, but the tears are close by. In order to heal, it is very important for us to allow ourselves to feel the pain and sadness. We need to grieve for what we have lost, and we need the healing that grieving brings. We need to heal so we can go on, so we can continue to live our lives, so we can move on. It is good to remember our past, but we must not live in our past. We must move on.

Perhaps it is helpful to remember that our loved one is in a better place. Do you believe your loved one is in a better place? Do you believe he or she is in heaven? Do you believe he or she is free of pain? Do you believe he or she is happy there? Here is what the Bible says about heaven in Revelations 21:4: *"And God shall wipe away all tears from their eyes; and there shall be no more death, neither sorrow, nor crying, neither shall there be any more pain: for the former things are passed away."*[2]

I believe my loved ones are in heaven. They loved and accepted the Lord, Jesus Christ, and believed in His word. I believe that they are no longer in pain. I believe they are happy in heaven and I believe that they want me to be happy too. I believe that they would want me to move on with my life. How about you? Do you believe, as I do, that your loved one is happy in heaven and wants you to move on with your life and be happy?

I also believe that our desire to marry again is a tribute to our loved one which says, "Being married to you was so good, I want to repeat the experience with another."

I believe that our wedding vows include the words, "until death do us part" for more reasons than just to keep a couple together to raise a family. They also release us so we can move on to build a new life with someone else with no feelings of guilt or regret.

A death in the family affects all its members one way or another. It sets off a chain reaction of events that have to be taken care of immediately; such as: notifying family and friends, making burial and funeral arrangements, changing account information at banks and other businesses, scheduling appointments with an attorney for the reading of the will, etc. The stress is enormous, emotions are raw and everyone in a loving family needs to be considerate and supportive of each other.

The surviving spouse's lifestyle has just been disrupted and suddenly altered forever and he or she needs the support of the other family members. This is the time to set aside petty annoyances with others in the family and to consider major decisions that the spouse now has to make. The family home may have to be sold, the spouse may have to relocate which will require time and physical help from everyone. Finances need to be discussed and a new budget plan may need to be set up because of less income. These are only a few of the changes which are now necessary. Remember that change is difficult at any time and it is even worse at this time.

What exactly happens during this period of grieving? Experts tell us that there are "7 Stages of Grief" that everyone goes through and I found it helpful to know about them. They are: shock, denial, anger, guilt, bargaining, sorrow and depression, and engaging life or acceptance.[3] The only stage I did not experience was the bargaining stage.

Shock and **denial** were my initial reactions. I had not expected him to die. When I heard the news, I gasped, "What? No! You are wrong!" How could I react any differently? This was a catastrophic event, and I was devastated. I accused myself of having killed my husband because I had signed the order for the intubation procedure that his heart could not take, and I had driven him to the hospital too late. Therefore, I was guilty. I had killed my husband!

Anger came later in the middle of the night as I tried to fall asleep but could not. Even though I knew my husband had gone to heaven and was no longer in pain, I hissed at him, "How dare you leave me alone now!" I raged, "How could you do this to me?"

Then **sorrow** came almost immediately too. I was sorry I had ever argued with him; sorry I had not taken him to the hospital sooner; sorry I had driven him to the hospital myself instead of calling for an ambulance; sorry I did not get to say goodbye or tell him once more that I loved him. Thinking about all of the "should haves" and "what ifs" succeeded in making me **depressed**.

At first, there was so much to do - planning the funeral, taking care of the guests, and packing for my move to Michigan that I did not have time to myself. But when all of those things were finished, the guilt returned, and I was depressed. I could not sleep although I was exhausted. I cried a lot and had no appetite. I lost ten pounds.

I had to force myself to get dressed in the mornings as I did not want to do anything or go anywhere. I kept chastising myself for having argued with him so much, telling myself I should have been a better wife. I forgot to take my medications. I was not taking care of myself. I missed my husband, and I was lonely.

When did I **accept** that he was gone? I still struggle with this at times. When I am busy at the computer (as we would sometimes do together), I get an idea and say to myself, "I have to go tell Bob." Because I was relocating, I was very busy as I tried to sell my Tennessee house and buy a new one in Michigan. All of that forced me into accepting my situation and participating in a new life. When I finished all the packing and the unpacking, I began looking around to see what my new community had to offer.

I volunteered to direct the church choir in an Easter Cantata. I went to the senior center and played cards. I checked out an online dating website and decided to discuss this option with my daughter. I traveled to visit my mother and sister in the Upper Peninsula, and then I flew to Colorado to see my brother. My mother passed away six months after my husband, and then it took seven months to settle her estate and to get her house ready to sell.

Listed below are other activities which may be helpful to you:

1) I cried. Crying is an important part of the grieving process and needs to be allowed because it brings relief. If you feel embarrassed or ashamed to cry, please don't. Please give

yourself permission to cry. Think about it this way, "God gave us tears to clear our eyes; and He gave us tears to wash away our sadness."

2)   Talking with someone. My friend John shared how a friend helped him: three months after his wife passed away he was at the grocery store and ran into a friend who said, "John, you look awful! Come, have a cup of coffee with me and let's talk!" He did, and that hour spent talking with this friend saved his life!

3)   Talking with someone is good therapy and helps both people feel better.

4)   Calling or visiting someone makes both of you feel better. We should all be so lucky to have someone stop by for a chat occasionally. Wouldn't it be awesome to save some-one's life by just giving them a chance to talk?

5)   Writing about the things that are bothering you on a piece of toilet paper and flushing it down the toilet will help you to forget about it.

6)   Writing your concerns on a piece of paper and placing it in your, "My God Box" helps also to put them out of

your mind. Years ago I saw this small, oblong box with the words "My God Box" on the lid at a craft show, and knew I had to have it. Surprisingly it helps a lot. Inside the lid is printed this verse:

When your head starts to worry,
And your mind can't rest,
Put your thoughts on paper,
And let God do the rest.

7) Did you know that in order to **help yourself feel better, you need to do the opposite of what you feel like doing?** In other words, when you are depressed, you feel like doing **nothing**. What is the opposite of nothing? **Something.** So, in order to feel better, you must do **something**. What is the **something** that you need to do? **Anything.** Therefore, to feel better, you must get busy doing something (anything).

8) Whenever you feel angry or upset: Set a timer for ten minutes and allow yourself to do whatever you feel like doing, such as: crying, yelling, hollering, screaming, pounding your fists into a pillow, etc. When the bell rings STOP! Go take a shower; shave or put on makeup; get dressed in something that makes you look good and feel good, and get out of the house! Go somewhere—anywhere!

SMILE at everyone you see! A smile is a gift you give to someone and usually they return the smile! Now two of you feel better! **Start talking to somebody**. They are probably lonely too and need someone to talk with them. Don't worry that you don't know what to say, or that you will say the wrong thing, just **open your mouth** and let the words come. The important thing is that **you are talking with somebody!** You are having a conversation. It feels good to talk to someone, and it makes the other person feel good too. You have just made a new friend. Isn't that wonderful? Repeat as necessary.

9) **Pretend** that you are **happy,** and you will **be happy!**

10) **Pretend** that you are **enthusiastic,** and you will be **enthusiastic!**

11) There is an old adage - Fake it until you make it!

12) Enjoy your memories. Our loved ones are with us forever in our hearts, and it is good to remember them. Allowing yourself to remember them and feel whatever emotion is evoked by their memory, is a good thing. Our memories are a part of us. We are who we are now because our loved ones were a part of our lives. It is right that we should

remember them. Some suggestions of ways to help the family remember a loved one include: plant a tree or bush in their memory in a prominent place in your yard; place a stone or other marker in your garden - mine is engraved with this phrase: "Those we love don't go away, they walk beside us every day"; at Christmas time place a chair in his or her memory in a prominent place or include a Christmas stocking with their name on it on the fireplace, etc.

13) Become active in your church or community, volunteering your time and help.

14) Taking a class that will get you moving and out of the house. I took up line dancing because it is fun and very good exercise. It has become my favorite activity, and I have made many new friends because of it.

15) Learning to play board or card games like Euchre or Pinochle forces you to get out of the house and helps you to make new friends.

16) Stop regurgitating! Does this word remind you of something unpleasant? It does me. First, it makes me think about cows in the field "chewing their cuds." But there is another meaning of the word: "to repeat (information)

without analyzing or comprehending it." [4] Does not that describe what is going on in our minds when we keep worrying or thinking about something over and over again and cannot get it out of our minds? I think it does and once this association came to me, I found that I can stop that process by telling myself to "stop regurgitating."

17) Write letters to your deceased loved ones and tell them how you feel, what you are doing and thinking, and whatever you would like them to know.

18) Our reactions to the challenges or sad times determine our future. We can choose to be negative or we can choose to be positive. However, if we want our future to be a happy one, then we must think positively and react accordingly.

19) Albert Einstein once said, "We **cannot** solve our problems with the same thinking we used when we created them." [5]

20) **Change** your thoughts. **Change** your actions. **Change** yourself. **Change** your life!

Chapter Three

THE DISCUSSION

A s the tears subsided and I began to think about my future, I decided that a friend might help me with my loneliness and I decided to talk with my daughter about a solution.

One evening when we were alone I began, "I've been thinking about something and I would like to ask your opinion. What would you think if I signed up for an online dating website?"

"What?" she replied. "Mom, you don't want to do that!"

"Why not? I am lonely, and I need a friend!"

"What? With all of this family around here?" she asked.

"Yes. Everyone has been wonderful, and I appreciate it. But you all are busy with your own lives. I have been here six months, and I haven't met anyone I didn't know before Bob died. I have gotten lost. I don't even know who I am anymore! How can I figure out what I want to do with the rest of my life when I don't even know **who** I am or what my options are?"

"Why don't you ask Kathy at church? She'll go out to lunch with you, I'm sure!" she said.

"I've already asked her, and she is busy with her garden and her family. She is worried about her heart and afraid to get too far from home," I answered.

"Well, you certainly do **not** need to go on a dating site," she exclaimed. "Why don't you go back to the senior center? You liked to play cards there, didn't you?"

"It isn't any fun there! Those people are out for blood. They only want to win," I replied. "I like to play for fun, but it is not fun playing with them."

"Mom, the men on those dating sites are not looking for a friend! They are not even real! They are. . .," she said waving her hands in the air, "out in cyberspace, the nether world of the Internet! They'll tell you anything, promise you the moon, rob you blind!" she continued. "You need to find real, live friends, and, while you're at it, stick to women friends."

I replied, "No one seems to want to be my friend around here! If I continue doing what I have been doing, I will never make any new friends. I have to do something different!"

"I just don't think you're ready to start dating again," she explained, "and besides, you are still grieving! I think you should wait longer before trying to date again! You don't remember how hard dating is! It was hard enough fifty years ago, and it is even worse now."

The conversation ended there, and I went upstairs to call my son. His reaction was very similar to his sister's, except he almost yelled into the phone, "WHAT? Mom you DON'T want to do that!"

So, I waited. . .

One week. . . Then I registered for my first online dating website.

What are my results so far? I have been a member of an internet dating website now for almost two years and, although it has been an interesting and fun experience, it has also been very time-consuming. Here are the results:

1) I have chatted with about three hundred men online.

2) I have actually met about fifty of them, and some of those have resulted in more than one date. Some have become good friends, and some have been a disappointment.

3) In comparison, I have met and dated only two men by traditional means.

However, I am here to warn you that many of the remaining two hundred men with whom I have communicated are "romance scammers." These guys set up fake profiles with stolen photos, pretend a fake relationship with their victims with the purpose of stealing their money, and they are extremely successful at it!

Be sure to read chapters fourteen through sixteen for more information and absolutely do not allow yourself to become a victim.

Do NOT send money to someone you meet online and guard your financial and other private information with your life. If you are already communicating with someone online who has asked you for money, or asks you in the future for money, end the communication immediately, block that person and report them to the authorities.

Chapter Four

DISCOVERING MYSELF

I don't know about anyone else, but after fifty years of marriage, I seem to have forgotten exactly who I am and what I stand for. I do not know what I want to do with the rest of my life.

In an attempt to find myself and decide what to do with the rest of my life, I began reading e-books and articles about men and women and relationships. I have included several of the thought-provoking exercises which I found helpful and I suggest you buy a notebook in which to record your thoughts and your answers to the questions provided in the next few chapters.

With so much negativity in today's world, how can we possibly think any other way? How many of us, women especially, tend to think negatively about ourselves and our physical attributes? If I were to ask you to make two lists: 1) a list of the things you like about yourself, and 2) a list about what you dislike about yourself? Which list do you think would be longer? Studies show that the second list is always much longer. Apparently we do not like ourselves very much.

We need to break away from all this negativity. Did you ever think about the creation and your part in it? Let's take a look at what Genesis Chapter One tells us:

In the beginning, God created the heaven and earth...¹
...God created man in his own image... male and female
created he them...² God saw everything that he had made,
and, behold, it was very good..." ³

It states that you and I were created in God's image! A few verses later state that we were created in the likeness of God! Think about it! We look like God! He was beautiful, don't you think? We read that six times God looked at what He had done and thought his work was very good. Everything God made was beautiful. Therefore, we are beautiful! Why should we think we are ugly? We need not think it, because we are beautiful.

The following exercises are designed to help us think about our positives. Why? Because we must love ourselves so that others will love us. It is time for us to learn to put our best self forward and it is time to become the person we were meant to be, the best person that we can be. Through the following exercises we are going to improve our self-image, find our strengths, and re-gain our self-confidence so that we can deal with our present and move on into our future.

Exercise #1: Standing in front of a floor-length mirror, ask yourself the following questions and then write your answers in your journal.

- Right now, am I the best person I can be?
- What changes in my appearance do I need to make to look the best I can look?
- What changes in my attitude do I need to make in order to become the best person I can be?

Perhaps you have heard the adage, "No one else is going to love you if you don't love yourself!" Loving yourself is important as it is the foundation for gaining a better self-image, becoming self-confident and achieving your desires.

Right now you are going to make a list of all those qualities about yourself that you **like.** I know that most people, especially women, spend a lot of their time pointing out their negatives, such as, I am too fat. Now is the time to stop those negative thoughts and find your positives.

Exercise #2: Take a full page in your journal, and write down all of the qualities that you like about yourself. Be sure to place the qualities in each of these three categories: Physical, Personality and Accomplishments. First, just list each quality (eyes, skin, etc.) and then write down why you like them. Here is an example:

<u>Physical</u> – I like my eyes because they are a vivid blue that changes to match the color of blue that I am currently wearing.

<u>My Personality</u> – I like that I am a happy person and can make my friends laugh.

<u>My Accomplishments</u> – I like that I have worked hard to earn my college degree.

Be sure to leave lots of room for each category; and completely fill the page. Resist writing a qualifier, such as: "I wish I were twenty pounds lighter." Qualifiers are not allowed.[4] Concentrate on your positives and forget about the negatives.

Exercise #3: When you are finished filling the page with your positives, the next activity is to take all those good things you wrote about yourself and turn them into a short, third-person paragraph about yourself, as if you were talking about someone else. Begin like this, "I like [<u>your name</u>], I really do _____, because she or he _____."[5]

I hope you completed those exercises. Make a copy of these three exercises and post it in a prominent place so you can read them aloud every day. Feel free to add to the list as you grow.

Exercise # 4: This next exercise was designed to help you re-discover and define your values. Our values give us purpose and direction. They provide us with a compass by which we can compare each new idea and help us to make quality decisions. They keep us from making bad decisions. They make decision-making easier because whenever faced with making one, we can compare and ask ourselves: "Does this action agree with my values?" If it agrees, then it is okay to do it. If it does not agree, then we do not do it.

Read and think seriously about each question, answering them in the order in which they appear and writing your answers in your notebook.

1. Suppose someone is giving a speech about you sometime in the future, what would you want them to say?
2. What would you most like to do if you had the time and money?
3. How would you define a true leader and the their leadership qualities?
4. What would you do if you knew that you could not fail?
5. Name two or three people who are an inspiration to you and why you think they are.
6. What would make your personal life more fulfilling?
7. What are the biggest changes you need to make in your personal life?

    a. If you decide to remain single?

    b. If you decide to find a new partner?

8. What activities do you most prefer to do?

9. What are your strengths?

10. What are you weaknesses?

11. Do you finish all of the projects that you start? If the answer is no, the why not?

12. What are you most satisfied with and what are you least satisfied with in your personal life?

13. Name three of your greatest accomplishments or achievements so far.

14. What is the hardest thing in your life you've ever had to:

    a. Overcome?

    b. Accept?

15. What two steps could you immediately take to make a big difference in your current situation?

16. Do you believe in God? Explain how and why.

17. Do you believe in yourself. Explain how and why.

18. What kinds of things drive you crazy?

19. If you had a magic wand, what would you change in your personal life?

When you are finished, go back to each question. Read your answers looking for and identifying your values and the deeper core value within each response. Get to know your strengths and your weaknesses, your likes, dislikes, wants, and needs. [6]

Note: You may want to add other thoughts to this list and/or change your answers from time to time. You will want to update it at times.

Chapter Five

THE DANCE BEGINS

How are you doing with your journey? Are you still sad? Are you asking yourself, "Is there light at the end of this tunnel?" Maybe you are wondering if the sun will come out tomorrow. The answer is, "Yes!" I know the future may look bleak at the moment, but as you work your way through your grief and think about the questions in the exercises, your self-image will improve, your self-confidence will grow, and you **will** begin to feel better. You can do it. You can teach yourself to think positive thoughts.

I chose "Learning to Dance in the Rain" as the title of my book because early in my journey I accepted the phrase as my motto. It has been the driving force that has motivated me to do all the things I have been doing these past two difficult years. When I told my friends the title of my book, several exclaimed, "That is exactly what you have been doing all this time!" The "rain" represents my sadness and grief at the loss of my husband and all the tears I shed. The "dance" represents the activities I have chosen to do to occupy my time, and the "learning" is the research and the application of what I have read.

My "learning to dance" has included many things such as: learning about and applying self-improvement tips, learning to line dance and to play euchre and pinochle, attending singles dances each week, playing the piano for nursing homes and church, and directing choirs. It also has included losing thirty pounds, buying new smaller clothes, changing my hairstyle and putting myself "out there" by signing up for several online dating websites. Learning to dance has been my therapy as I worked toward building a new life for myself.

Do you know what you want in your future? Do you want to remain single and enjoy that lifestyle? Do you want to start dating again and searching for a new life partner? How does one decide which lifestyle suits him or her best? Perhaps the questions in **Exercise #5** will help:

- Am I positive or negative about meeting someone new?
- Does my heart feel ready for a new partner?
- Why would I want a new partner?
- Why would I want to stay single?
- Am I happier being alone or with others?
- What are my major priorities right now?
- Do I have time to get involved with another person?
- Have I allowed myself to heal and grieve following my loss?

- Do I want to date just one person, or do I want to play the field?
- Are my emotions under control?

Relationships take a lot of time and energy and are not always easy. Our emotions can run from extreme highs to extreme lows quickly. Remember how exciting it was to be "in love" in the beginning? Do you also remember how it felt when things went wrong? I think of dating and falling in love as similar to riding a roller coaster. At first it is exciting and fun. It feels good to like someone who likes you back. But life has a habit of allowing twists and turns and complications to arise which allows our doubts and insecurities to surface, and then it is not so much fun after all. We wonder: *Did I say something wrong? Did I do something wrong? Is something wrong with me?* The negatives always stir us up and our imaginations can run wild. We begin to regurgitate (our thoughts) and we become depressed.

After talking so much about becoming positive and self-confident, I apologize for bringing up some negatives, but I want you to know that the negatives will come. You will be faced with negatives and with rejections, and you need to have the self-confidence to deal with them. Some ways that I have learned to react to a rejection is to say, "NEXT!" and to remember the saying, "When life gives you lemons, make lemonade." Then I continue my dance.

Be sure to take your time making your decisions about your future. There is no rush. It is better to relax and take your time.

Never attempt to force a relationship. God's timing is not always our timing. We need to be patient and focus on our positives, enjoying each day as it comes. We need to go about living in a natural and pleasant way, keeping ourselves busy, active, and prepared. God is working for us in the background.

Consider the advantages of living a single lifestyle: you can go where you want to, when you want to, and do whatever you choose to do without consulting anyone else. There is no one telling us what to do. We can enjoy each day and make it a good one.

Suppose you decide that you want to find a new partner, where does one go to meet available singles? How does one start up a conversation with someone new? How does one go about attracting someone he or she might like to get to know better? What does one have to do to be more attractive?

Let's consider the meaning of the word, "attract." According to http://www.vocabulary.com, to attract means "to exert a force that draws something in, like the way a magnet attracts a paper clip." [1] Does this mean we must make some changes in ourselves in order to become a people magnet, to make ourselves attractive? The answer is probably yes. How do we do this? What qualities attract other people?

According to the Business Insider, an American business news website, "There are five scientifically proven ways in which a man is attracted to a woman. . ." [2] It goes on to say that everyone could benefit from incorporating these attraction magnets into their daily living. What are these attraction magnets? They are:

1. **Laughter** – People are attracted to others who are happy and fun to be around. A woman who is receptive to a man's sense of humor and laughs at whatever he thinks is funny, plays into his need to be respected and connects with him on a deep level. I believe that the reverse is also true, that a man who appreciates a woman's sense of humor will also be attractive to her.

2. **Smile** - There are forty-three muscles in your face, and when you smile, your body releases neuropeptides called: dopamine, serotonin, and a whole mixture of feel-good chemicals, which make you feel good. Usually the person receiving the smile, will smile back, thus releasing their own feel-good chemicals.

3. **Honesty** – An honest person is a confident one, and both of these qualities increase your attractiveness.

4. **Wearing red** - Sexual attraction and desirability are increased when a woman wears something red. However, the article suggests that if red is not your color, then wear another powerful color that is attractive on you.

5. **Mirroring a man's body language** – This is a good way to build rapport with a man. The article suggests that when a man is telling you a story and leans in to you, then you should also lean in to him. If he sits back and puts his hand on his face, you do the same. If he shows he is getting excited, then you need to show excitement also. When you

are able to mirror him, then you are becoming more con-nected with him. [3]

My comment on #4 is that I never used to wear red because I thought it was not my color, but as I have gotten older, I began to incorporate the color into my wardrobe and I have since noticed that whenever I wear something that is red, more people smile at me and speak to me.

Statement #5 seems to be a bit extreme and perhaps contriving. To me, being actively engaged in listening to the other person is more important than actually mirroring him.

To be attractive one does not have to be extraordinarily beautiful or handsome, but one must look nice and presentable by wearing neat and clean clothing and having well groomed hair and makeup for the women. Looking good adds to a person's self-confidence, and confidence is another turn-on for both men and women. Other qualities that are attractive and contagious are being enthusiastic, energetic, independent, happy, and interesting. No one wants to be around a negative or "needy" person.

Once a couple is attracted to one another and begin to spend time doing things together, they may begin to develop a strong feeling for each other. How do they know if this is love or something else? How do they know that they are they falling in love?

According to the Oxford Living Dictionary, love refers "to the intense feeling of deep affection one person has for another. . . Love is a <u>deep romantic feeling</u> for, or a <u>sexual attraction</u> to someone." [4] Everyone keeps reminding me that love is not immediate, that it takes time to grow and develop.

What is that attraction or strong feeling we have, if it is not "love"? Everyone tells me that "a spark" or "chemistry" is only lust and that lust doesn't last! According to the Oxford Living Dictionary, "Lust is a very <u>strong sexual desire</u> that one person feels for another." [5]

Very interesting! Both definitions contain the word "sexual" and I must confess I was surprised when I noticed that. Then I remembered that the two phrases: "having sex" and "making love" are interchangeable.

Can it be that lust is the magnet (attraction) that draws two people together and the love (or bond) that develops becomes the glue that keeps them together?

I am thinking the reason for so many divorces today is because a couple gets married thinking they are "in love" when actually they are "in lust." Once the lust fades, they think they need a new partner in order to get that "spark" back. Love is forgotten because it did not have time to develop. Love is what keeps us together when things get tough. Love is the glue. Love is the commitment, or the promise we make when we say our wedding vows to "love, honor, and cherish until death." The word, commitment, seems to have become a "bad word" lately. Many people don't want to commit to anything anymore. Will the word, love, also become a "bad word"? I hope not. Perhaps we need to remember the biblical definition of love:

Love is patient, love is kind. It does not envy, it does not boast, it is not proud. It does not dishonor others, it is not self-seeking, it is not easily angered, it keeps no record of wrongs. Love does not delight in evil but rejoices with the truth. It always protects, always trusts, always hopes, always perseveres. (I Corinthians 13:4-7, NIV) [6]

Just in case you would like to know more about this subject I have included the following three lists which answer the age-old questions that I have encountered about "How do we know we are in love? How do we know that we are loved?"

The first list was written by Theresa E. DiDonato, Ph.D., a social psychologist and associate professor at Loyola University Maryland, who claims the following signs will help a person to know he or she is in love:

1. You are addicted to a certain person. You want to be with them all the time.
2. You really want your friends or family to like this person.
3. You celebrate this person's triumphs (even when you yourself fail).
4. You definitely *like* this person, and this person likes you.
5. You really miss this person when you're apart.
6. Your sense of self has grown through knowing this person.
7. You get jealous—but not suspicious. [7]

DiDonato continues: "If *love* is passion, security, and emotional comfort, *commitment* is the necessary decision made within one's cultural and social contexts to be with that person. . . .people who watch romantic comedies know that love needs the buttressing of commitment to flourish into a stable and healthy partnership." [8]

This second list was written by Sabrina Alexis and gives eleven signs for a woman to tell if a man loves her:

1. The way he looks at you.
2. He wants to give to you.
3. He treats you like a priority.
4. He wants to immerse himself in your life.
5. He really sees you. He doesn't just love you, he loves things *about* you
6. Your happiness is as important to him as his own.
7. He misses you when you're apart.
8. He keeps you in the loop.
9. He's there for you even when it's inconvenient.
10. He doesn't give up.
11. You don't worry how he feels—you just know. [9]

This third list, "Does She Love Me? 15 Signs She Actually Loves You," compiled by Bella Pope, https://everydayknow.com, helps a man to know if she loves him:

1. She supports your passions.

2. She wants to get to know your friends.

3. She's pleasant with your family.

4. She compliments you all the time.

5. She's passionate about you.

6. She's patient with you.

7. She's eager to discuss the future with you

8. She openly communicates with you.

9. Your arguments are had with the intention of fixing the issue.

10. She doesn't try to change you

11. She does the little things for you.

12. Her friends have taken an interest in you

13. She's not judgmental toward you at all.

14. She compromises with you.

15. You just feel it. [10]

Chapter Six
MEN AND WOMEN ARE DIFFERENT

Yes, men and women are very different and in several different ways. At times it seems that we are from different planets. Sometimes it even seems like we are speaking different languages. Men tell me they don't understand women, and I know I don't understand men.

Carlos Cavallo, www.datingadviceguru.com, is a relationship adviser who has worked with thousands of men and women, and has recorded several audio courses on dating and relationships which I have purchased. My favorite is entitled, "Understanding Men." Cavallo claims that "most women have it all wrong about men." [1] I find his information to be enlightening and I have obtained his permission to share some of it. Carlos's words are within quotation marks which I follow with my own comments.

First, Cavallo asks: "Suppose your man has a good reason for what he does. . .? Suppose he is genetically programed to act a certain way and cannot change his behavior. . .? Could this (knowledge) make a difference in your reactions to his behavior. . .? and would (this knowledge about men) make a difference in your relationship?" [2]

I pondered these questions, thinking about my fifty-years of married life, and I have concluded that things would have been different in my relationship with my husband had I known some of these things when he was alive. It seems to me that our arguments always started with a misunderstanding, followed by my getting my feelings hurt because he was not doing or saying what I thought he should be doing or saying. I think had I understood some of the following things about men, I would have handled the situations much differently. Following are some examples:

"Men are not wired to think about two or more things at the same time and are unable to multi-task." [3]

I never realized that most men simply cannot multi-task as I can. . . I guess I just never thought about it because it is second nature to me. However, Cavallo suggests that understanding this one concept will allow a woman to plan ahead and, therefore, avoid interrupting him when he is working on a project. She could then schedule her "want to talk times" at a more convenient time for him. Some bad times to attempt a conversation with a man include whenever he is watching the news or a sports event, whenever he is reading, and whenever he has just gotten home.

Women do have the innate ability to multi-task and it is this quality that enables them to take care of the kids while fixing dinner, and to talk on the phone while paying the bills, etc.

"Men are direct, saying exactly what they mean. . ." [4]

I do not agree with this concept because I know men sometimes say the direct opposite of what they really mean just to test a woman's reaction. Even later in the same e-Book, Cavallo contradicts his own statement by advising a woman to look at what a man <u>does</u> rather than what he <u>says</u>. Men also have totally different meanings of some words and will use them in totally different ways than a woman does. Therein could lie the reason for misunderstandings between the sexes.

I agree that women have the tendency to be indirect, sometimes hinting at things rather than saying what they mean.

"A man **is** his opinion and disrespecting his opinion is disrespecting him!" [5]

I have come to realize that this statement could very well be true because it seems that several men I know ended our conversation soon after I expressed an opinion that was different from their own. Also, I notice several men on the dating websites are quite close-minded on certain subjects and even write into their profile statements like: "I am a liberal, and if you are not, please do not contact me." Another thing that supports this statement is the fact that once a man has made up his mind about something, it is almost impossible for him to change it.

"Men have a stronger sense of self than women do." [6]

I agree that women tend to be wishy-washy and indecisive more often then men and I attribute this to the fact that they are more concerned about what others think about them and are sometimes afraid they will lose their man if they disagree or express their true opinion. However, there are men who are also insecure and have poor self-images just as women do.

"Men fall in love more quickly than women." [7]

I was surprised by this statement and I think most women would be also. However, when we stop to remember that men are visual creatures who tend to pay more attention to the way the woman looks than to other details, it is easy to see that he can fall quickly for a beautiful looking woman.

A woman, on the other hand, while she may be attracted to a man's physical appearance, she tends to study his personality to see how he acts so she can determine if he will meet her needs.

"Men want to be appreciated." [8] Women also want to be appreciated. However, little boys do not get praised for good behavior like little girls do. Boys are likely to be thought of as "trouble-makers," usually told to "suck it up" and be strong. A woman needs to remember to tell her man that she appreciates him, but she must also be truthful about her praise for a man knows when he is lacking in this department.

"A man wants three things: a. to be helpful, b. to solve problems (fix things), and c. to feel useful." [9]

My response to each of these three things is as follows:

a. I know that my husband wanted to be helpful around the house. But, by being overly critical and telling him where he had failed to measure up to my standards of cleanliness, I destroyed some of his motivation and desire to help me. I learned too late that sometimes it is better to allow a man to do whatever he is willing to do and not to judge him or his results. Just accept the help he gives.
b. My husband was definitely a "fixer." He enjoyed fixing things around the house, and whenever I just needed to vent, he always offered a solution to my problem.
c. As my husband grew older and became physically unable to fix things around the house or do the jobs he once had done, such as: yardwork, driving the car, etc., he felt useless, degraded and embarrassed.

"A woman wants a man who is educated, has ambition and wealth, is respected, has some kind of status, is tall and strong, dominant, assertive, has strong facial features and a good sense of humor (which shows intelligence, novelty, and flexibility), and willing to make a commitment." [10]

My women friends and I came up with quite a different list of what we wanted in our man. We want him to be caring, honest, understanding, thoughtful, clean, handy, old-fashioned, a gentleman, and a good dresser.

"In short," Cavallo claims, "men want a sex object and women want a success object." [11]

What can I say about this? It seems to be the truth.

"A man will never be able to love a woman like she wants him to love her." [12]

A man loves differently than a woman does. A man wants respect and to him love is respect." [13] A man shows that he loves a woman by providing for her, protecting her, doing things for her. A woman needs to know that a man shows his love by what he does. He is showing a woman he loves her when he offers to help her. Can you let a man help you?

"A man wants to make a woman happy and if he thinks he cannot make her happy then he will leave her alone." [14]

I was surprised to hear Carlos say this but I have recently become aware that it might be true.

"Men are born hunters. They love the chase and they love to win." [15]

Experts all agree that men are meant to be the chasers and they emphatically advise women to allow the man to be the chaser. This is why it is a complete waste of time and energy for a woman to work hard to please a man, thinking it will make him love her more, because in fact, it is what drives him away. In other words, a woman needs to find ways to make her man work for her love.

My favorite of all the relationship books I have read is Steve Harvey's, *Act Like a Lady, Think Like a Man*. It is easy to read, and enjoyable. Harvey claims:

"A woman who genuinely wants to be in a committed relationship. . .must be able to understand what drives a man, what motivates him, and how he loves. If she does not understand these things, then she will be vulnerable to his deception and to the games that he plays." [15] Harvey admits that the game a man plays is to do whatever it takes to get the woman he approaches to sleep with him. [16]

The following concept is for women only. Cavallo claims that the biggest mistake a woman can make and one that causes a man to immediately start running in the opposite direction is to be the first one to say, "I love you." [17]

I think the reason for this is because he has not yet decided how he feels about her, and when she says these words, then he knows he has her and he begins to feel obligated and/or trapped. He knows he has won, and he must begin another hunt.

What a woman needs to do instead, is to remind him of how he benefits because of her. In other words, she needs to tell him, in a subtle way, what's in it for him to stay.

Here is a woman's **Exercise #6**: Make a list of how a man benefits because of you. Then at the appropriate time, you will be prepared to tell him one of these benefits. I admit that when I was writing my list, I could only think of sex, cooking, laundry, and cleaning. My good friend, John, helped me to list some more. Below is **our** list:

1. I am your "eye candy," and you are proud to show me off.
2. I am a very good companion.
3. You enjoy doing things with me.
4. I am fun to be with.
5. I make your life fun.
6. I like to do things with you.
7. I like to go out with you.
8. We like to do spontaneous things, on the spur of the moment.
9. I look attractive, and you enjoy watching me when I don't know it.
10. You enjoy watching me in action.
11. I listen when you talk.
12. You enjoy our conversations.
13. I am good company.
14. You enjoy traveling with me.
15. I show you that I appreciate you.
16. I tell you that I admire you.
17. I encourage you, and you feel like a better person when you are with me.

18. You like physical contact.

19. You like me to touch you.

20. I like you to touch me.

21. You like to cuddle with me.

22. I like holding hands in public and while watching television.

23. You feel better when we are together.

24. You like the way I make you feel.

25. I understand you.

26. I "get" you.

27. I make you feel safe.

28. I allow you freedom to be with your friends occasionally.

29. I allow you to maintain your independence.

30. I help you with chores.

31. I allow you to "help" me.

32. You like it when I allow you to do things for me and vice versa.

33. I prepare good meals for you.

34. I keep your house neat.

35. I help you with your laundry.

36. I help you with our finances.

37. I help you to have a fun social life.

38. I help with your decision-making.

39. I accept you and your differences as a man.

40. I understand where your thoughts come from.

41. I know what drives your desires and influences your emotions.

42. I connect with you on your level.

43. I know how to keep you attracted to me and I use it wisely.

44. I work to build the kind of connection with you that we both want.

This is a good time for the men to make a list of the qualities they are looking for in a woman, and for the women to also make a list of the qualities they are looking for in a man.

Chapter Seven

DATING IS DIFFERENT TODAY

"Dating today is different," my daughter said, and she is right. In general ways it is the same, but the times have changed. We have changed. Our goals, attitudes, wants, and needs have changed. When we were twenty, we were looking for romance and someone to marry so we could build a home and have a family. Today we have our families, and, hopefully, we are financially secure. However, some of us still want romance. Many of us want companionship and someone to do things with. We still want to have fun, preferably with someone we like.

Many of us have "issues" caused by our experiences of the past fifty-plus years and some of us are set in our ways and may be unwilling to make the necessary changes and compromises that living with a new partner will require. Our loving adult children may feel the need to protect us and may object to our finding a new partner. Our bodies may not be able to do the things we once did and still want to do.

Some of us still want to love and to be loved, and, yes, some of us still have sexual desires. After being accustomed to our needs being met as needed or wanted over the past fifty years, how does one deal with these needs? We must learn to control ourselves or find other ways to meet these needs. This is certainly a biggie today while playing the dating game. We senior women want to do know whether a man's equipment still works, and the men want to know if a woman has any interest in the activity.

Society has changed. Today's culture looks at sex, marriage, and living together much differently than it did fifty years ago. Things once kept private are now out in the open and discussed openly everywhere. Today a get acquainted interview can result in finding out if both partners are still interested in having sex, as well as a discussion about prostate cancer, sex toys and oral sex.

We are now faced with very dangerous results of careless sexual activity. Age does not protect us from sexually transmitted diseases (STDs) and (STIs), and all of us must educate ourselves and learn how to protect ourselves from them. According to WebMD, "In 2012 the rate of sexually transmitted diseases (STDs) has more than doubled among middle-aged adults and the elderly over the last decade. . ." [1] It appears that these middle-aged adults think they are free from worries because they cannot get pregnant. However, there are worse things than pregnancy that can happen to us today.

The following information comes from the website, www. webMD, and everyone needs to do their own research to learn how they are impacted and how they can protect themselves. Here I have paraphrased a short introduction:

> Sexually Transmitted Diseases (STDs and STIs) used to be called venereal diseases (VD) and they are among the most common contagious disease in the world. More than sixty-five million Americans have an incurable STD, and each year, twenty million new cases are reported. Half of these infections are among people ages fifteen to twenty-four and all have long-term consequences. The germs that cause STDs hide in semen, blood, vaginal secretions, and sometimes saliva. They are most often spread by sexual intercourse, including vaginal, anal, or oral sex, and include just about every kind of infection. [2]

Chapter Eight

HANDLING OBJECTIONS FROM ADULT CHILDREN

A huge obstacle to our moving on with our lives appears to be our own adult children. Many seniors have found that their kids do not want them to find new partners. They don't want to think that their parents still have sexual desires. There seems to be no end to our children's selfishness in regard to their parents' time or money.

Many seniors have found it necessary to step up to raise their grandchildren when their own children have become ill or died, and, in these situations, they should be praised. However, many other seniors are being taken advantage of by their children who refuse to grow up and become responsible adults themselves. Too many of them have become accustomed to the lifestyle provided for them by their parents and expect them to continue filling their financial gaps.

My friend, Jim, suggested that I warn seniors that they need to think of their own financial needs now instead of spending their money or giving it away freely to their adult children and grandchildren. He tells me that he has met a number of women who are in financial difficulty because of their generosity to their kids and now find themselves destitute and desperate to find a man to support them. Please do not let this happen to you.

I heard Suze Ormand, a Financial Advisor, tell people years ago that instead of saving for their children's college education, they need to be saving for their own future retirement needs. The children must learn to support themselves and to pay for their own college education. Once seniors retire, they will be living on a fixed income trying to pay for expenses that will be increasing. Seniors must learn to say "NO" to all requests for their money because they are going to need it themselves. If they do not take care of themselves first, seniors will not have the finances to pay for their own needs.

Assisted Living facilities already run over five thousand dollars a month and will continue to rise. $5,000/month times twelve months equals $60,000/year. Multiplying that by five years brings the total cost at a minimum to $300,000. How does that compare to your retirement funds? Are your children going to have the funds to take care of you? Think about it.

According to an online article found on www.eHarmony. com, senior adults "have every right to meet new people, start new relationships, and to build a new life." [1] They should never allow anyone to discourage them from dating, if that is what they want to do.

The article continues, "There are two reasons why your adult children object to you finding a new partner, time and money!" The bottom line is that the kids are **jealous** because your new relationship is taking your time and **money** away from them." [2] A serious talk is needed in which you can assure them that you love them and will continue to make time for them. This is also the time to inform them of the contents of your will or trust. This is not the time for secrecy.

The article lays out the following questions to ask the kids so you can learn the real reason behind their objections:

a. What would you like to achieve with these negative feelings?
b. What effect is my new relationship having on **our** relationship?
c. Do you think your attitude and behavior are going to affect my relationship with the person I love?
d. What would you like to see happen?
e. Let them know that you are upset by their behavior, and you are torn between wanting to please them and wanting to move on with your life. Tell them that you need to move on.
f. Ask them to give your partner a chance and, if they refuse, try to keep your two relationships separate.

g. Change takes time and, hopefully, when they see you enjoying life again they will accept your decision.

h. If nothing else works, just ask them, "Don't you want your mom (dad) to be happy?" [3]

It is natural for your kids to want to **protect** you from getting hurt emotionally or financially, but now is the time for you to put yourself first! If you don't do it now, it will never happen. Remind them that they have their own lives to live, that they enjoy intimacy and that you are no different from them.

Genesis 2:24 tells it all: *"Therefore, shall a man leave his father and his mother, [adult children?] and shall cleave unto his wife: and they shall be one flesh"* KJV. [4]

Chapter Nine

ABOUT ONLINE DATING

There are many ways to meet other singles and according to www.datingsitesreviews.com, here are a few statistics for 2018:

58% of singles meet dates through friends.

37% meet dates in bars, coffee shops and other public areas.

27% meet in the workplace and or at events.

27% meet through their hobbies.

49 million people in the United States have tried online dating.

46% of dating app users met their current partner online.

46% of people have a positive attitude towards dating services.

19% of adult singles in the US say they are registered on a dating service." [1]

I like how Michael Fiori describes online dating in his e-course, *"Online Allure,"* and I am quoting it here:

Online dating "sucks" because. . .

- Guys are only interested in sex and not a real relationship;
- Scammers from Nigeria use online dating to prey on innocent women for money;
- Guys lie on their dating profiles;
- Dick picks;
- When nobody sends you a message you feel rejected and lose some self-esteem;
- Crazy guys asking you to marry them before they even meet you;
- You get stuck in email hell with guys who refuse to meet in person;
- You meet someone you really like and then find out he/she is married. [2]

Online dating is awesome because. . .

- You don't have to get dressed up or get drunk to meet a really nice person;
- You can set up a profile to be your magnet getting people to approach you while involved in actually living;
- Great people are often shy and scared to actually walk up to a stranger in the real world and ask them out. Online dating provides a safety net and opportunity to relax and flirt with someone;

- There is a wider selection of possible candidates to choose from; and
- The #1 reason is because online dating actually works! [3]

I have entered Fiori's description of the "Five Kinds of Men on Online Dating Sites" [4] into the chart below:

Five Types of Men Online Dating Sites:	Goal 1	Goal 2	Goal 3
1: The sex shopper	Sex	Sex	Sex
2: The commitment addict: To be avoided because they are often emotional physical abusers and are extremely jealous	Ego Gratification	Control	Sex
3. Scammers: To be avoided they are liars and cheats	Money	Money	Money
4. Nice guys/really good guys: majority of men on the web fit into this category. Shy guys are often great guys but they are lacking in self-confidence. They have incredible approach anxiety and are scared of women in one way or another. They are often frustrated and even a little angry, and they use online dating because it allows them to talk to girls without the fear of talking to them in person.	Sex	A Girlfriend	Companionship

5. The alpha male: Has plenty of confidence, takes up space in the room, has an effect on women, and usually dates multiple women at once because he can. He is charming because he has had lots of practice. He has a job or owns a business or feels powerful in his everyday life and is incredibly attractive. He also is incredibly frustrating to women, in short, he is a "player."	Sex	Ego	Vague about the Future

If you have any computer skills and a desire to find a companion and/or lover, I encourage you to try online dating. As my friend John says, "It is an interesting activity in the evening, better than television, and you meet and talk with some very interesting and entertaining people."

The dating websites all have their own safe and secure text messaging and chat platforms which the members are advised to use. If you receive a message asking you to use another method of communication than what is offered by these websites, you should tell them you prefer chatting on the website for a while until you get to know them better. Most people will understand and those who do not are most likely scammers and you do not want to chat with them anyway.

You do not want to give your personal information to a criminal and a liar, whose only goal is to steal your money. Be safe and utilize the secure means of communication provided by the dating websites. It is very important to be careful and statistics reported to the website, www.datingsitesreviews.com, claim that "there are on average 25,000 scammers online with victims at any one time. . ." [5] The report also claims that "500,000 of the 3.5 million profiles it scans every month are fraudulent." [6]

Be safe and stick to the dating website while getting to know someone on the internet.

How does communication take place on the dating websites? To answer that question, I have quoted the following definitions from the Wikipedia Online Dictionary which gives a short history of the means of communication we use today.

"**Text messaging** is the act of composing and sending electronic messages between two or more users of mobile devices, desktops/ laptops, or other type of compatible computer. Text messages may be sent over a cellular network. . . or via an Internet connection. The term originally referred to messages sent using the Short Message Service (SMS). . . but has grown to include. . . digital images, videos, and sound content, as well as ideograms known as emoji (happy faces, sad faces, etc.)." [7] Text messaging is a quick and easy way to communicate with friends and colleagues when the two people are not required to be present at the same time. It was first used in 1992.

"An **E-mail** is a text document which is sent to your Internet Service Provider server when you press the 'send' button. There it sits for a little while, from a few microseconds to an hour or so, whenever the mail server batch process outgoing email. This document is transmitted as a single file, including attachments, to another server, the recipient's Internet Service Provider's incoming mail server. . . The message then resides on the incoming server until it is downloaded by the recipient." [8]

"**Instant text messaging** is a series of data packets, sent as the "send" key is activated, which are routed whichever way is available, to another computer. However, many ISP text servers are operated in a batch processing fashion, so the text messages may sit in the outgoing server for a second or two." [9]

"**Online Chat** is a conversation between two or more people at computer keyboards. . . sent without delay, to each computer that is logged into the chat session." [10]

"Email is fast, text messaging is faster, and on-line chat is the fastest." [11]

On a dating website, communication begins whenever one person sends a message of interest to another. The recipient receives an alert text message and then must log into his or her account online to read the message and respond accordingly. I suggest checking your messages frequently because good conversations can take place if one responds right away while the other person is still online. Otherwise it can become very frustrating to wait for days or weeks to get a response and to get know each other.

Always observe proper etiquette when responding to messages while in the presence of a third party. Most of the time it is rude to carry on long text conversations in front of another person. I try to quickly read my message and send a short reply telling the sender I cannot "talk" right now. If a longer reply is needed, I excuse myself and move to another room, just as I would with an important phone call.

However, observe how your friends handle their calls and text messages and that will tell you how to behave in front of them.

Be sure to read your message before you send it. Sometimes the auto correction app writes things you did not mean and it could be embarrassing.

Chapter Ten

GETTING STARTED WITH ONLINE DATING

You will need to research the dating websites to find the ones that will best serve your needs. A website called, www. DatingSitesReview.com, lists most of the available dating websites with their details. Be sure to check it out and then choose two or three websites you think will serve you best. Your goal is maximum exposure. I suggest paying upfront for the six months subscription as that is the best value.

Your personal webpage is called a "profile," and it will contain your information. You want your profile to catch the eye of a quality person who matches the description of yourself and your interests. You will enter your age, height, education level, profession, interests, and whether you are a "woman looking for a man" or a "man looking for a woman." Be sure to save your answers before going on to another page.

You will be asked to write a short **description** about yourself. Tell a little about the kind of work you do, what you do for fun, what you are passionate about, a little about your personality, and a little about what you are looking for. Show your confidence, and keep it light and fun! Be sure to save your work.

You will need to upload some **photos of yourself**. Be sure that one of your photos shows you smiling at the camera. Another might show you actively involved in something you like to do. Do not include photos of you with other people, and no animals unless you are in it and very visible. Nude and other suggestive photos are not allowed. Besides, you are a quality person, and a quality person does not do such a thing.

Once you save your work, you are "live" and everyone who matches your criteria can see your profile and you can see theirs. You are the "new kid on the block" and may receive a deluge of messages at first. I was flattered and a bit overwhelmed in the beginning and it seemed to me that I fit perfectly the description of what most of the men were looking for. However, I soon found out that all of them didn't agree with me.

It is important to remember that you are a quality person and that you want to attract quality people, so please do not include words that make you appear "needy." Do not use the following phrases: "Princess looking for my prince" or "I didn't want to do this so my sister (or brother) signed me up." Never participate in sexy talk.

As soon as you have chatted with someone enough to tell that you are interested in meeting them, try to schedule a short meeting. It is suggested to do this within the first two weeks of chatting. However, I have found it difficult to do that. Fiori advises that if you cannot get a meeting within two weeks, then move on.

When scheduling a meeting always remember you are vulnerable and need to protect yourself. You could disappear and never be heard from again. Always think safety first and set your boundaries as follows:

- Schedule the meeting in a safe, public place;
- Leave a written message in plain sight at your home stating where you are going and with whom and any information you know about your date, including his/her full name, telephone number, car description, license plate, etc;
- Be safe! Drive yourself to the meeting place and, should you decide to go somewhere else, drive yourself there also! Do not get into your date's car; and,
- Ask for the model and color of their vehicle, then look for it in the parking lot.

Fiori also gives the following tips to keep in mind as you read profiles and messages.

1. **Block** anyone who goes sexy in the first message, appears to be a scammer, obviously has not read your profile, does not answer your questions, or sends you a message that is insulting or hateful; [1]

2. **Warning signs** on a guy's profile include: pictures of himself with other women, shirtless pictures with his guitar, badly-lit pictures, and use of poor grammar and misspelled words; [2]

3. If you are **asked no questions**, then you are not having a conversation, so forget them! Seventy-four percent of singles identify good conversation as the single best indicator of great chemistry on a date.[3]

4. If the message sounds **strange**, do not open it; it is probably a scam.

5. **No Response** to your message? It is not a big deal. It could just be bad timing. It is not about you! Wait at least two weeks before writing the same guy again. [4]

6. It is okay to take the initiative if you are a woman.

7. Just because one guy isn't interested in you does not mean you aren't interesting! Remember this is a game! Say, "Next!"

8. **Bad response?** You do not have to respond. It's not about you. [5] Don't force the issue. Cut the cord and move on. Stay positive and relaxed. Ignore the rejections.

YOU DESERVE THE VERY BEST!
DO NOT SETTLE FOR ANYTHING LESS!

According to the first study for 2018 made by the dating website, Zoosk.com, most of its members are looking for love and romance and they state that by including the phrases, "old-fashioned" and "hopeless romantic" to your profile, you will generate more responses. [6] It is worth it to include them in your profile.

Chapter Eleven

BEWARE OF SCAMMERS

B eware of the romance scammers on the internet who are after your money. It has become a multi-million dollar illegal business and people are losing their lifetime savings to these criminals. Be very careful and do not become one of their victims.

Is your name on a "Suckers List"? Have you sent money to a beautiful young Southeast Asian woman who asked you to send her an iTunes card or wire her some money? If the answer is yes, then my friend, you are a "victim" and your name is now on a "Suckers List." How does that make you feel?

Have you fallen in love with the photo of a handsome, successful-looking American business owner working in a foreign country who has experienced an emergency and has asked you to wire him some money? Did you send it to him because he tells you that you are beautiful and he loves you? If the answer is yes, then you are also a "victim," and your name is on the "Suckers List." How does that make you feel?

Once your name is on a "Suckers List," your information is shared with other scammers and you will be contacted again in the future for more money. To avoid being put on this kind of list, you must be careful and you must refuse all requests for money. Once you familiarize yourself with the red flags I have listed in the next chapter you will be able to recognize a scammer almost immediately. Once someone on the internet asks you for money, then you know for sure that you are chatting with a scammer and you need to block them immediately and stop communicating with them. You also need to report them to the owners of the website on which you met this person. Whatever you do, do NOT send them money or accept gifts or money from them.

According to the FBI, romance frauds are the second largest of all scams and there have been more than a million victims in the US. Although there has been a lot of media coverage warning about these scams, there is an epidemic of vulnerable adults giving their money away to these criminals, and there seems to be no end to it. In 2016 the FBI claimed that, "Almost 15,000 complaints categorized as romance scams or confidence fraud were reported. . . (nearly 2,500 more than the previous year), and the financial losses associated with those complaints exceeded $230 million. . ." [1]

According to Wymoo International Investigators report, "Romance scammers are experienced criminals. . . who understand the game they play better than anyone. They are especially dangerous. . . Every word in the conversation is planned (and recorded) so there (are) no inconsistencies. . . Everything is calculated so that no one. . . can uncover the fraud." [2]

These scammers are polished professionals who utilize professionally written scripts designed to win the affection and trust of their victims. Widows and widowers are a major target because of the assumption they have lots of money from recent inheritances. American men are susceptible to beautiful young women who plead for gifts of money or iTunes cards.

A former scammer testified that he had earned an average annual income of over $200,000 "taken" from only a handful of victims.[3] Do you make that kind of money? Do you still feel sorry for those pretty young women because you have money, and they do not? Think again because most likely they are wealthier than you are.

Many of us rational adults cannot understand how other adults can fall for these scams, but the fake scripts appear to be real and lonely people are convinced with "brain-washing" techniques and become almost hypnotized into giving away or loaning their money. Only later do they "wake up" to discover they will never get their money back, nor will they ever meet the scammer.

Because of the privacy of the internet, the authorities are unable to stop this criminal behavior. I have begun to think that the only way to stop it is for all of us to make our own war against them by spreading the word so people will stop giving away their money to these liars and cheats. If the scammers cannot make money in this manner, why would they continue to try?

Currently, the criminals are winning, and we, seniors, are losing the battle as more and more of us become victims. We must stand together, develop our backbones and just say "NO!" to these requests for our money. End this epidemic, and we save ourselves. The only reason criminals are winning so far is because we are losing. This losing streak of ours must end!

Please pass on this information to all the people you know and meet, and if you are chatting online right now with someone who sends you beautiful love letters and exhibits other warning signs of a scammer (see my next chapter), stop talking to them immediately. BLOCK them and report them. If you are the victim of a romance scam, file a complaint with the FBI's Internet Crime Complaint Center immediately.

Absolutely do not send money to anyone you meet online! Whatever story they have told you, it is a lie! Say NO and BLOCK them immediately!

Dr. Phil McGraw had a lady on his show recently who is absolutely convinced that she is married to the actor, Tyler Perry. She has already given him one hundred thousand dollars out of her retirement account. Her daughters brought her to the show hoping Dr. Phil could convince her she was being scammed. Dr. Phil introduced Karla as follows:

"There's one hitch to this fairy-tale romance; she's never even met the man she calls her new husband!" Dr. Phil received an urgent anonymous email claiming the clock is ticking for Karla who's blowing through her retirement fund to please her online love. Karla's lost her job, house and friends, and alienated family members, and has even lost custody of her two younger children. Her two older daughters, Kelly and Kourtney, join their mother to get her to face the truth about her digital marriage dilemma with the help of Dr. Phil." [4] (https://www.drphil. com/shows/my-mom-is-delusional-she-thinks-shes-married-to-tyler-perry-and-has-sent-her-catfish-100000/).

Even though Dr. Phil presented Karla with proof that she is the victim of a scam, she is so sure of her romance that she refused to believe him. Please do not allow this to happen to you. Trust your instinct. Your gut feeling tells you a lot. Listen to it. Always **listen to your head, NOT your heart**.

If you suspect in any way that you are talking to a scammer, immediately stop communicating with him/her. Block him or her immediately! **Do not threaten or bait them.** These are very dangerous people. If you encounter one, immediately report him/her to the website.

1. Realize that you can and must say no to anyone requesting money, whether you know them well or not;
2. Remember the old adage: If it sounds too good to be true it probably is;

3. If you are having a conversation with anyone and recognize any of the red flags, or warning signs, in the next chapter, stop chatting with them and block them on your cellphone immediately;

4. Love takes time, time spent together doing things and talking in person;

5. Things are not always the way our minds visualize them or the way we want them to be;

6. Ask yourself, would a real man ask you for large sums of money? NO! Most quality men would rather die than ask a woman for money.

7. Online dating can be an exciting and successful journey of exploration and ecstasy, but you need to educate and protect yourself.

8. Be diligent in looking for these red flags (warnings) in the next chapter.

9. Listen to your intuition, your "gut," and your head—not your heart.

If you have sent money or been targeted with a request for money by someone on the internet, notify your local authorities immediately, so they have a record of your incident.

We must stop giving criminals our money! We must stop this epidemic!

Chapter Twelve

RED FLAGS TO RECOGNIZE A SCAMMER

S cammers follow a pattern. They use template letters and messages with a few changes and they send them in mass mailings of emails, texts, and chats to see who will respond. Each scammer is easily recognizable once you learn the warning signs or "red flags" and you will be able to spot them almost immediately.

Some of the red flags listed below can be found on each of the dating websites and/or in a Google search. The rest I have discovered for myself. Feel free to make a copy of this list and post it near your computer. Always read through the profiles and messages looking for any of these signs or red flags before responding.

1. Distance - more than seventy-five miles away is too far;

2. Too great an age difference: it is not realistic for a twenty to forty year old to want someone sixty or older;

3. Scammers are usually self-employed businessman; engineers; off-shore oil rig workers; military;

4. Anyone traveling and/or working outside of the US;

5. Widowers or divorced with a school-aged child;

6. An older man with a young child, i.e., a seventy-two-year-old man with a six year old daughter;

7. A photo of a person who looks younger than the age shown on their profile;

8. Perform a Google Image search to see if it is a copy;

9. Beware if you are asked to move to a communication platform different than on the dating site. Such as: Private email, text, Google Hangouts, etc. for any reason;

10. Notice any inconsistencies such as: their profile says Indiana, but their telephone number has a New York area code;

11. Backgrounds in their photos can sometimes confirm their location or disprove it.

12. Background Search to confirm their information;

13. Do they have a Facebook page with just a few friends or photos?

14. Do they have a Twitter or Linked-In account? Check the information on both.

15. Do they make plans to visit you then cancel?

16. Do they profess almost instant feelings of love for you by sending beautifully written poems and emails, and/or links

to love songs on YouTube, or cute and lovable emojis and images in their chats?

17. Do they ask you for money or an iTunes card?

18. Do you receive very similar stories from different suitors? This indicate the use of templates.

19. When talking on the phone, do they have a foreign accent? Are you able to understand what they are saying?

    Explanation: *Does your phone reveal an area code that does not match their stated location? If you call them, does a live person answer the phone? Do they sound like they are "in a box," or are there echoes?*

20. Run a background check as soon as possible, if you cannot find the man then he is not giving you the truth. Get as much information as you can including the man's full name, city and state, telephone number, and email address so you can research that information. As soon as I can, I want to call the number he has given me because I want to find out the answers to these questions:

    (1.) Who answers the phone? Is it a real live man, a woman, or an answering machine?

    Explanation: If a man answers, then we have a conversation. But if I get a recorded message such as, "This text messenger device owner is not receiving calls at this time. . ." then I have a red flag because this person is keeping his identity a secret, and I want to know the reason!

(2.) If a man answers, does he have an accent? Can I understand what he is saying? Is his voice disguised in some way?

Explanation: If I cannot understand him because of the accent, then conversation is too difficult, and I end the conversation. Additionally, this is a red flag.

(3.) Is there background noise? Does his voice echo or sound like he's in a box? Are there people talking in the background? These are all red flags.

(4.) Does a woman answer the phone when I am calling a man?

Explanation: If so, he may be married.

(5.) Have I heard this voice before?

Explanation: If the answer is yes, it is a scammer!

21. Anyone asking the following questions:
    a. How long have you been on the dating site, and what has been your experience?
    b. Do you live alone?
    c. What are you doing now?
    d. Where are you going?
    e. Have you eaten breakfast (or lunch or dinner)?

22. If they call you by the wrong name or misspell it then you know they are a scammer;

23. Watch to see if their spelling and grammar deteriorate after a few messages;

24. If they ignore your questions;

25. If they tell you they make a six-figure income or more, or they own several expensive homes; and

26. If they tell you to stop communicating with others on the dating site right away.

Chapter Thirteen

YES, I AM A VICTIM

Yes, I am a victim of a scammer. Yes I sent money to a stranger on the internet even though I had promised I would never do that. Scammers are very good at what they do. The stories they tell can really play on a person's heartstrings, almost hypnotizing them into handing their money over to them.

In this chapter I share the stories of the men who have tried to scam me. I have changed their names to protect myself but I printed the emails as I received them. I have copied and pasted their exact words so you will know immediately that you are chatting with a scammer if you receive one like these. You will also see how their grammar and spelling deteriorate over time. Some stories I have told rather than printing because they are so similar.

My first scammer was Gerry, from Ohio. He was the first to ask for my email address "so we could get acquainted faster." Gerry never got around to asking me for money, because my background check on him proved he was a liar. However, I have printed here only a portion of his three-page email to me.

Hello_____,

let me start when my wife (T.) and two children, K. & B. passed away... My wife was from the Caribbean (Cuba) and unlike most American men, I married for love not tradition. I remember going out with her for six months before we made love. When the exciting day came, she asked me what took so long, and I said I wanted to be sure that we were both ready for it at the same time and that nobody would be hurt. I guess I made an impression because one year later we were married.

The day that my family was killed, 01/18/2000. In the morning it started to snow... I had gone to work that day in the morning where I worked in NYC at a very prestigious firm.

As the day was progressing the snow was falling harder. The firm decided to give everyone off, so I went to the train station to take the hour and 15-minute ride home. Before going home, I stopped the jewelers to pick up Theresa's present, an engagement ring that I promised myself that I would buy her. I came home to find the house empty, with a note stating that Theresa and the children were out doing some last-minute shopping and that they would be home soon. I was young, 46 years old because I was born in

'September', dark hair, kind of thin, with a full beard. About three in the afternoon there was a knock on the door. . . I opened the door to find two policemen standing outside they asked if I would accompany them to the police station with me. I went with them to the police station. . . .

The story continued with more details about what happened at the police station and the death of his wife and two daughters. He also described a relationship he had several years after the accident which revealed how old-fashioned and chivalrous he was. I chatted with him for two days before I thought about running a background check on him and found that he had lied to me. His report showed the names of his daughter who had died in the accident and they were still living. I blocked him.

However, a year later from a different dating website, he again came up as a match for me and he sent me the same messages, and I again sent him the same email address, wondering if he would recognize it. He did not because I soon received a shorter version of the above letter minus the women's names. I could not help writing, "So nice to hear from you again, Gerry, but it seems you have forgotten our conversations of a year ago." That was the end of that.

My second scammer was Robert from Orland Hills, Illinois. We had been matched through an extensive questionnaire by Dr. Fisher on www.chemistry.com. Robert claimed to have a PhD in Marine Engineering and at the time of our communication he was the chief engineer in charge of a submarine headed for the Southeast Highlands to make a delivery of goods. He could not tell me his exact location or destination for security reasons. He wrote that he liked my profile and my photos and claimed the age difference did not concern him, as it was just a number. He was fifty-nine to my seventy-five. He was an excellent writer and his grammar and spelling were perfect, but there were several red flags including 1) he was a self-employed professional traveling outside of the US; 2) he professed love for me almost immediately; 3) he sent me love letters with cute images and links to his favorite love songs; 4) he told me to stop communicating with others on the dating site so we could concentrate on each other; 5) he was irritated with me when I told him I would not fall in love with anyone I had not met in person; 6) he did not like my answer to his question about whether I "loved unconditionally" or not, and 7) He ignored most of the questions I asked of him.

Because I suspected right away that he was a scammer, I played along to see just how long it would take him to have an emergency and ask for money. The answer was two weeks. There was an emergency in the engine room and the submarine was "dead in the water," and he needed me to purchase a part to fix the engine because a hold had been put on his credit cards. The part cost twenty-thousand dollars to purchase and have airlifted to his location. He became very upset with me when I refused and began pressuring me to change my mind because he was afraid the pirates would attack and kill him and his crew and steal his shipment. Finally, I realized that I did not have to listen to this garbage and blocked him!

My third scammer was Eugene from Coldwater, MI, who claimed to be a business man leaving on a quick buying trip to China. This was to be his last trip before he retired. At the end of the second week of chatting with him, a Chinese dock worker fell and died while loading Eugene's purchases on a ship. Eugene's story became more and more real as he told me that his passport and all his money had been confiscated by the Chinese police who told him he would have to pay money to the dead man's family. Every day, the amount of money he required increased. I was emotionally drawn into this story and there seemed to be no solution to his problem. He was trapped in a foreign country and starving to death because he had no money to buy food. I became so upset that I called a US government agency and reported the incident to see if there was a solution to this problem. I was told it was a scam.

I believe this guy was also attempting to involve me in a money laundering scam because he wanted my address so he could have his attorney in the Netherlands send a package supposedly containing his inheritance from his mother's estate to my house and, once I received the package, I was to take out whatever the amount of money was that I had sent to help him get out of China.

About a year after all of the above happened, I saw his profile and photo on a different website. He had not even changed his name.

Isn't it wonderful that he made it back to the US without my money? I wonder how?

My fourth scammer was Charles from Georgia who sent me a friend request on Facebook. Charles proved to be one of the group known as Oil Rig Scammers. I recognized several red flags almost immediately and it soon became evident that he wanted me to launder some money for him by accepting it in packages sent to me which I was to deposit in certain bank accounts around the US. When I realized what was going on, I blocked him immediately and stopped communicating with him.

My fifth scammer was Charley of Chicago, Illinois, which I met through e-Harmony. He claimed to be a construction manager with a bachelor's degree in engineering. He sent me a nice photo of him with his sixteen-year-old son. He told me that his wife had left him, and he had been hurt badly. His mother lived with him and took care of his son in his absence. He said that my profile showed I was the one he wanted. I ran a background search on him and found no report. This was the first red flag. Soon after that I spotted another red flag when I received a message from the e-Harmony telling me that Charley's account had been terminated because of fraud. I forwarded the message to Charley, and he replied that he didn't know why some people had been telling lies about him and he hoped I would love him enough to believe him and trust him, so we could continue to get to know each other.

Next, he told me he had won a contract for a job in Egypt and had to leave right away, but that he would return in a few weeks and then we would meet and hopefully get married. A week or so after he supposedly landed in Egypt, a large piece of equipment broke and he asked me to wire him some money. I blocked him.

Several months later, I decided to call his cellphone number to see who would answer. Charley answered, and when I identified myself, it shocked me when he responded, "Do you have the money for me yet?" I ended the call and immediately blocked him again. I certainly wasn't expecting that response!

Military Scammers is another group of scammers pretending to be in the service of their country and wanting to become friends. Three of these guys almost immediately began talking about sex and so I blocked them right away. Two others I chatted with for a while until I decided to find out if there were men pretending to be in the military who had asked for money or other favors. I found out that there is a website that lists the names of all people who really have served their country in this way, so I entered the two names that I had and discovered the names were on the list. However, I also discovered the dates of their deaths.

The following message is obviously a template because I have received it from about many different email addresses. Do not click on any email link that you do not recognize.

Hello, this is S. . ., I'm sorry for just getting back to you. I got a message from you on the dating website. The website seems to be no luck for me, and I have been out of town for vacation. Also, I don't get notifications on new messages from the site in a very long time, that way -I missed getting back to you.

Now, I'd like to know more about you too. I had to renew my membership just to get your address and requested for a cancellation. Please get back to me. You seem to be courteous and I really like your profile. Please, I really want to get to know more about you and let's find out where the chemistry takes us. You can follow here to check my profile on the dating site. Regards, S. . .".

The following sentence is used quite frequently and is a red flag. *"My late wife was a loving woman before she met her untimely death. . . now intending to move on with my life with that lovely, honest, faithful woman with so much love to give because I am tired of public settings with dishonest, unfaithful People."*

One of my potential scammers tried to convince me he was not a scammer by sending me a photo of his passport stamped with the country he was supposedly in at the time. It is a template, so don't fall for it!

You are undoubtedly questioning my sanity by now, wondering why I subjected myself to all of this. At times I have asked myself the same thing, but then I reminded myself that I wanted to know what would happen if I did not follow the websites' advice to decline giving out my personal email address and that I planned to write this book. Therefore, I needed to do my research.

I have talked with many people who want nothing to do with online dating, and my experiences probably confirm to them that they are correct in their decision. However, I have only written about the "bad guys," but there are many, many good guys online as well.

I continue to think that online dating is the best way for me to meet available single men and I intend to continue my search until I find the one I am looking for.

How does online dating compare to meeting someone in the real world? My results are that I have chatted with three hundred men so far, and I have met and dated fifty men, some more than once. In the real world I have dated only two men that I met at the singles dances. I prefer the odds for online dating. Because of my subscribing to online dating websites, I have a very full social life, and I have had a lot of fun in spite of the scammers. I enjoy meeting people and all of my dates have included stimulating conversations. I do not regret having met any of these guys. I have been stood up only once and that was on the day of the time change last Spring. I have a lot of good memories that I would not have had otherwise. I have been disappointed only a few times, but I have had more than my share of rejections. I have learned a lot and made several very good male friends. I am a survivor and I know each rejection brings me that much closer to finding my one and only.

In the future I have decided to follow my advice about relaxing and allowing God do the work for me. When I started my search, I anticipated that I would find my true love within six months or so and was surprised when some of the men told me that they had been on the dating sites for several years. At the time I wondered what was wrong with them, and now that I have spent twenty months at it, I sometimes wonder what is wrong with me. However, when I told my friend John that, "Maybe I am just too "picky", he response made me feel good, "No, you are selective."

What a nice man! I would not have met John, who has become such a very good friend had it not been for online dating. I would not have wanted to miss meeting this man (even if I have never met him in person) for the world. Both of us agree that we have a strong and unique friendship!

What was it I said a few chapters back? Oh yes, **"Remember you are a quality person, and you are looking for a quality person!"**

I know that it is difficult for most people to understand how anyone can be taken in by these scammers so I decided to share the following letters to show how a lonely and vulnerable woman can easily fall in love with a stranger. I have to admit that these letters made me feel so good that I looked forward to each morning to see whether I would receive another or not and to see just how long it would take before the writer would request money from me.

I have not printed all of the letters but those I have printed are quoted verbatim as I received them, except that I italicized the quotes to make it easier to see my comments.

On June 3, 2018:

"Hello, dear. . . I'm not quite sure what I'm supposed to tell a complete stranger. But here goes nothing. Your beautiful and you were something. What matters in life is who you are and what you're doing with your life. Made mistakes? Redeem them live the good life so far continue to do it. Don't let people bring you down or make you feel worthless because they are far from right. After viewing your profile, I got so impressed that I have to send you this message just to indicate my genuine interest as I was encouraged to try the dating site by my mom who is tired of seeing me lonely of which I was finally signed up by my daughter.

I am well-balanced, listen well, young at heart, funny, love to laugh, have healthy sense of humor, patient, financially secured, genuine, independent, show passion, honest, and can be trusted. I enjoy a variety of things to do and always like to experience other opportunities. I love the beach so much and it's always fun to walk in the cold beach sand barefooted. I will have to say that the high agent my profile is a mistake as my daughter made an error when registering me on the site of which I could not figure out how to fix the age issues. So, I am a healthy 64 years old man and I do not believe that age or distance is a barrier to a loving relationship as what matters most is the love and beauty inside.

Of course, I would <u>really love to get to know you</u> well and also tell you more about myself as I want you to feel free to write me directly to my direct email contact:____ or you <u>can send me your own email</u> contact as for me to write you first if that is what you want. Why I am giving my email to you is because I am not regular on this site as I am not too familiar with the social media knowing that I am old-school type of person and hope to meet after a couple of emails. I hope to hear from you soon enough so that we can open a direct communication and get to know each other better. Wishing you all the very best at the moment. . . Cheers! Kind regards" James

Is that not a beautiful message to receive? How could I not respond to it? James's photo on his website profile showed a very attractive businessman wearing a white shirt and a red tie, sitting at his desk in his office. There was a filing cabinet with a VW emblem on the side. It looked very official to me.

The only red flag is in the last paragraph when he asks for my email address so quickly. I asked myself, Wow, is this guy for real?

Be still my heart. At this stage of the game, there is no way to tell if "James" is his real name or if the photo is of him. But I responded, "Hey There :-)" James replied immediately, "Hey how r u. Nice to have you here."

As we chatted, I saw several red flags as follows: 1) Construction business; 2) He just won a contract in a foreign country; 3) He was leaving the next day; 4) He has a young daughter; 5) He asked me to move to another website for our conversation; and 5) He plans to retire when he gets back to the US.

Having received similar stories from several scammers, I know that all I have to do is wait for the emergency and the request for money. I tried to speed up the process by writing, *"You have to think about a lot of things. I hope you are prepared for any emergencies."* He responded, *"Honestly I am doing the very best. I heard Taiwan is a difficult country. And I am preparing is much as I can."*

Later he wrote, *"Hey S___, what makes you this beautiful woman you are? I so admire and want the very best for you."*

I replied, *"Thank you."*

He wrote *"You're welcome; what can I ever do to make you happy for the rest of this life?"*

This conversation continued in a similar fashion for several weeks. He told me about his challenges at work: getting enough workmen to do the job, problems trying to obtain the lumber and other required materials, and as he became tired, he wrote less and less and finally stopped altogether. I don't know what happened to him.

On July 22, 2018, I received the first message from Alex. He did not request communicating off the website for several days, and there were few red flags in these letters. Finally, after five days we exchanged email addresses because where in the beginning he had wanted to take it slow, he was now falling in love with me and wanted to write longer letters. As I write this it has been five weeks since we began messaging, and he has not yet mentioned an emergency or requested money. I have printed only a sampling of these because they are each three to four pages long or more, but you can get an idea of the hypnotizing and believable effect a stranger can evoke within a vulnerable and lonely woman. Is he a scammer or not? I do not yet know. This has lasted twice as long as any other of my communications:

Letter #5, July 27, 2018:

"Hello Dearest, how are you today? I hope this email finds you on a loving mood. I want to thank you for the email and the almighty for giving us another day. I had to wake up this early to send you this email because I have been thinking so much about you and I will be having a very busy day so I need to get this off to you now. Like I said in my first email to you; though I will like to take this relationship slow, I will like to be positive. My giving you my heart at this point does not mean that I am trying to rush it rather I am being positive and consistence so forgive me if it seems that am

taking the wrong step. . . Let me say here that going on line to find a suitable companion seemed hopeless for me at the beginning. Most of my earlier contacts that wrote stating that POF suggested my profile to them as a MATCH were from much younger women so I could not understand how I could be a match to a 37 years old woman when I stated what I wanted on my profile. They always left me feeling bewildered and asking the questions - should I be flattered or insulted? In addition, there was always the concern - "what were the motives"? My faith was restored, when I decided to write instead of wait to be written; I wrote you and you appeared I thank my "lucky star" and enjoy the wonder of it. Essentially, I was so deeply happy that you displayed the qualities I was looking for. I found out that we shared a lot of the same interests and I adored the expressive e-mails. When I emailed you, I told you that I looked at your profile for over 30 minutes and you must be wondering what I saw during that 30 minutes that made me email you. I have come to realize that lonely times make us search harder for the good times. Bad times are only vague memories and we can look to the future with optimism to happy times. To "give" and "receive", to pamper, to spoil, to guide, to care for in all ways, makes for a wonderful relationship. There is no need for anger, when there is understanding, loyalty and sincerity, open communication and the ability to compensate for differences. Life is meant to be enjoyed and thus, should not harbor hurtful thoughts and actions. . . They say "Love" overcomes all obstacles. But to love blindly - leaves scares in your heart. The "ups" and "downs" in people's life's can be painful but can be healed with limitless compassion. Mine is healed so let us heal yours if it is still there. If your heart has been damaged too much by some cruel evil man, I can help you fix it like I fixed that of my late wife. If you have lost a partner like me, I can still fix it like I fixed mine or let's say, we can fix ours together.

When I say we can fix ours together, I know that Life isn't always a bowl of cherries. Based on this fact, I have decided that I need a woman that is not looking for someone to make her happy, but rather someone to share happiness and experience life's adventures and sometimes tribulations. You will agree with me that everybody need happiness both man and woman. Happiness is created in many ways - mostly in what people do and say! Your words can encourage me to drink long and hard from the cup of life; to capture every drop of adventure that comes my way.

I often ask myself, why we met - even if it was in such an unconventional way! I truly believe that a "path" is mapped out for us, when we are born. Are we given a purpose - are we given instructions on how to live our life and what we are to achieve? We are guided by our parents, teachers and friends and unconsciously adapt some of their ways to our life. However, there is a greater plan for us in the making. We are tested daily to make us stronger. Stumbling blocks are put in our way to overcome and make us rise above them.

Many people travel from cradle to grave without ever seeing themselves clearly, without accepting heartache and grief and without ever wondering about their past, present and future. They accept their life blindly, without questions or true understanding of their own value and potential. They become frustrated, disillusioned and bitter. We have all been given the tools to excel, feel more important, more fulfilled and more useful. You have shown me that you know how to use the tools so don't ever let anyone tell you that you will not accomplish and excel at what you have chosen, or perhaps, what had been chosen for you. What measure do they use to compare, or do they feel inadequate in their own achievements?

. . .So, was I meant to come into your life to help you see your own worth, to encourage and support and show you the heights that you have already accomplished. I have not chosen your "path" and don't know the plan decided for you,

but I know you have a passion for life, so you are and always will be successful. I am grateful to you for giving me your trust, but I think you now know, I would not misguide you.

When I think about you, a picture comes to mind, a woman sweet and gentle, with a heart that is one of a kind. Your light shines ever bright - your love an endless sea. . . . and nothing could be sweeter than the love you would have for me. I see you as my inspiration, but most of all God's Gift to me". I want to wish you a happy day and with this email welcome you to an inspiring day of good luck and success in all you do. This letter may not be too romantic but inspiring enough to start your day with a new relationship. I thank God above for you. May you always find new blessings for as long as you may live. . . Hugs! Hugs! It's me; Alex

Letter #6: July 29 at ten forty-five in the morning:

I must confess that it was such a joyful and pleasant moment with you on the phone yesterday. Though it was a short conversation for me, but I was actually feeling like a young teenager receiving his first call from his high school girlfriend. . .lol. You sounded pretty tender, smart, and intel-ligent and most importantly I really enjoyed the fact that we both talked peacefully and laughed together. That alone has showed me that you would be so much fun to be with! I will try to call you today. I want to hear more of your sweet voice, but then again, I can't wait to see you soon!

I want you to know that you are presently making me the happiest man on earth again by putting these handsome smiles on my face every morning that I wake up... You are always on my mind...

I want you to know that my day starts when I receive your wonderful e-mail, and ends with me sending you a reply. That is why I do wonder why you are in my thoughts all the time? The in between time is filled with romantic notions, breathless anticipation and a million and one thoughts of how our first meeting will go. Will there be fireworks will there be balloons in the sky? I know I am fantasizing, like a foolish teenager, but it makes me feel young and so extraordinarily happy.

I must confess that I have tried to suppress the feeling of calling you my love all this while to avoid looking like I am rushing everything but each time I want to email you, it keeps coming into my mind. It is a known fact that I am falling seriously in love with you and cannot stand not seeing you soon. You have brought this change and joy in me that I believe has attracted this lifetime business luck to me. Meeting you brought the breakthrough that I have been struggling to have with the investor for almost two years.

All I want you is to understand my situation and take me the way you see me. It's not that I fall in love easily but having been alone for over seven years makes me want you as soon as possible. All that I am sure is that this is not lust or a game of days but a life time relationship. I was married to my wife for 26 happy years and she was my first and only marriage. That alone will tell you more about me.

Please bear with me if I use those words so early. It's due to the way I feel that make me write the way I do. You are an angel in disguise. . . . you have touched my heart thus making a difference in my life. Bringing more Joy and success than you will ever know that you have done. . .

I think of you every moment of the day and I wish that at the end of a very hectic day that you will be there my side. I need you so much. I want you to know that the first day we knew over the computer, I knew you were the one for me. It is almost two weeks now and we are still fondly in each other's minds, souls, and hearts. Before I met you online, I almost forgot what love really was until my heart truly started aching for you. Each day we are apart, tears ran down my face unconditionally for the longing of you near me. I never knew a woman could have stolen my heart again and made it truly hers. I never knew I could love a woman more than my own life.

I long for the day I can finally look into your beautiful soft, kind eyes and tell you how much I miss you, and need you. What I need to survive and make it through this lonely world can only be conquered with you by my side because it was really a great battle with line during my seven years of loneliness. I do not think there are any words that could describe the way I actually feel about us. We will plan our meeting before I return back home. All I know is you, Darling you are the only woman that is in my mind, the only woman that is in my soul, the only woman who truly and unconditionally has my heart for my life time and many more lifetimes the world has to offer us.

When I think about you, my eyes start to water because I know you are somewhere else and not in my arms. But the thought of you keeps me going and going for another breath of fresh air to keep my longing for you in my life going. I will never leave, and I will truly never hurt you. . .

I am aware of all your dreams and wishes. We shall accomplish them as great couples. We shall always have the best of time to share together. I have never met someone that is as intelligent as you are in recent years. You are my dream come true. What can I even do without you? Thanks so much for making me fall deeply in love again. You are my perfect match. I hope you are enjoying the new day over there.

Darling, I am scared of tonight because am so sure am not going to sleep but think about you always. You are the best thing that has happened to me in recent years and I am very proud of you. I see myself as the luckiest man on earth to have you as my darling and friend. Please thank you so much. Take care Alex"

August 9:

My Darling, Thank you for your email and your concern over my mother's illness. It has not really been easy for me not being able to communicate with you or at least write you an email. I had to go out to an internet café to be able to send you this email. I couldn't go for two straight days without looking at my email knowing very well that there may be an email from you waiting for me. . . .

I want you to know that I have really missed you and was so happy when I opened my email and there was a mail from you! I can't wait to be with you. I can't wait to look into your beautiful eyes and tell you how much I love you! I can't wait to hug you at the airport! I can wait to touch your face and plant a long kiss on your mouth! I can't wait to give you all, I can't wait! I can't!

    With love, Alex.

Can you read these love letters without your emotions being set in gear? Do you wonder, as I do, if this man is for real or not? Do you know if he is a scammer or if he the man of my dreams? So far, I am unable to tell. Yes, I am the one with twenty-months experience, and yet I do not know what reason he had for this communication. I see only two red flags: 1) He had to go abroad on business, and 2) He fell in love with me very quickly.

On August 16, Alex wrote that his mother had died and two days later I received the last letter from him in which he expressed his pain and extreme sorrow. I have not heard from him in over a month. What was his motivation for sending me these letters? Was he just playing me for fun? He never requested any money. These letters were different from any others I have received, and I do not know what to make of them.

Chapter Fourteen

WHAT IF?

I watched a movie, *Letter to Juliet,* on television the other night, and near the end I knew I had found the perfect ending to this book. The main character read a letter describing a true situation but suggesting the audience consider what could have been. In other words, **"What if?"**

Two words: *what* and, *if.* When used separately each word has its own meaning, but when used together, the phrase means something else entirely. [1]

According to Oxford Dictionaries, *what* asks for information specifying something, or asks for a repetition of something not understood; [2] and *if* introduces a conditional clause, on the condition or supposition that; in the event that. . . It also introduces a hypothetical situation. [3]

However, when used together they ask: *What if I had chosen that path instead of this one? What if he changes ? What if I had not missed that plane? etc.*

Robert Frost's most famous poem, "**The Road Not Taken**," deals with this dilemma.

Two roads diverged in a yellow wood,
And sorry I could not travel both
And be one traveler, long I stood
And looked down one as far as I could
To where it bent in the undergrowth;

Then took the other, as just as fair,
And having perhaps the better claim
Because it was grassy and wanted wear;
Though as for that the passing there
Had worn them really about the same,

And both that morning equally lay
In leaves no step had trodden black.
Oh, I kept the first for another day!
Yet knowing how way leads on to way
I doubted if I should ever come back.

I shall be telling this with a sigh
Somewhere ages and ages hence:
Two roads diverged in a wood, and I,
I took the one less traveled by,
And that has made all the difference.[4]

I recall several incidents in which I told my husband, "Let's come back here someday!" Most of the time, we didn't get to go back a second time. That is why we need to enjoy each day as it comes, and to make each one a good memory.

Look into your future, which path will you choose now? Will you go back into your past and choose the "path not taken" years ago? Or will you accept my challenge of being single or a new romance? It is up to you.

What if you meet the person of your dreams and live happily ever after?
What if you have a happy life living single?
What if you take that trip to Australia that you have been dreaming about?
What if you don't?

Now is the time to do what you want to do and to go where you want to go. If not now, when?

May God bless you and keep you and help you to find whatever it is that you seek.

The End (or is it?)

NOTES

1. Vivian Greene, *Goodreads Inc*, (2017), Accessed August 21, 2018, https://www.goodreads.com/quotes/132836-life-isn-t-about-waiting-for-the-storm-to-pass-it-s-about.

Chapter Two

1. Dictionary.com, s.v., "grief," accessed September 7, 2018, http://www.dictionary.com/browse/grief.
2. The Holy Bible, KJV, Revelation 21:4.
3. Blaise Pascal, *"7 Stages of Grief,"* Journeythroughgrief.com, http://www.journey-through-grief.com/7-stages-of-grief.html.
4. Regurgitate, s.v., "regurgitate", accessed October 31, 2018, https://en.oxforddictionaries.com/definition/regurgitate.
5. Albert Einstein, *Brainy Quote,* accessed June 21, 2018, https://www.brainyquote.com/quotes/albert_einstein_121993.

Chapter Four

1. The Holy Bible, KJV, Genesis 1:1.
2. The Holy Bible, KJV, Genesis 1:27.
3. The Holy Bible, KJV, Genesis 1:31.
4. Michael Fiore, *"The Magnetic Online Dating Mindset,"* Online Allure, Module 1, Lesson 2, http://digitalromanceinc.com, 2013.
5. Ibid.
6. Marni Kinrys, "Turn Yourself On in Order to Turn Him On," *That's Not How Men Work,* (Venice, CA, 2017), www.thatsnothowmenwork.com, 65-79.

Chapter Five

1. Vocabulary.com, s.v. "attract," accessed, September18, 2018, https:/www.vocabulary.com/dictionary/attract.
2. Kevin P. Ryan, the Business Insider, Axel Springer SE, 2009, https://www.businessinsider.com/.
3. Ibid.
4. Oxford Living Dictionaries, s.v. "love," accessed August 20, 2018, https://en.oxforddictionaries.com/definition/love.
5. Ibid, lust, s.v. "lust," accessed August 20, 2018, https://en.oxforddictionaries.com/definition/lust.
6. The Holy Bible, NIV, I Corinthians 13:4-7.
7. Theresa E. DiDonato Ph.D., Psychologytoday.com, accessed October 31, 2018, https://www.psychologytoday.com/us/experts/theresa-e-didonato-phd, 2018.
8. Ibid.
9. Sabrina Alexis, "11 Undeniable Signs He's In Love With You," A New Mode, accessed October 31, 2018, https://www.anewmode.com/dating-relationships/signs-he-is-in-love-with-you/5/, 2018.
10. Bella Pope, *"Does She Love Me? 15 Signs She Actually Loves You,"* accessed October 31, 2018, https://www.everydayknow.com/does-she-love-me/, 2017.

Chapter Six

1. Carlos Cavallo, Audio: *"Understanding Men,"* accessed May 1, 2018, https.//www.datingadviceguru.com, 2017.
2. Ibid.
3. Ibid.
4. Ibid.
5. Ibid.
6. Ibid.
7. Ibid.
8. Ibid.
9. Ibid.
10. Ibid.
11. Ibid.
12. Ibid.

13. Ibid.
14. Ibid.
15. Steve Harvey, *Act Like a Lady, Think Like a Man,* First Ed. (New York: HarperCollins), 2009.
16. Ibid. Harvey.
17. Ibid. Cavallo.

Chapter Seven

1. WebMD.com, "*Understanding Sexually Transmitted Diseases (STDs),*" accessed August 19, 2018, http://www.webMD.com, 2017.
2. Ibid.

Chapter Eight

1. eHarmony.com, "*Dealing with Objections to your New Relationship from your Adult Children,*" accessed August 21, 2018, 2017, https://eharmony.com/dating-advice.
2. Ibid.
3. Ibid.
4. The Holy Bible, Genesis 2:24 and Ephesians 5:31, KJV.

Chapter Nine

1. Dating Sites Reviews, accessed September 20, 2018, https://datingsitesreviews.com.
2. Ibid. Fiore, "*Online Dating Heaven, Online Dating Hell,*" Online Allure Module 1, Lesson 1," accessed April 24, 2018, https://digitalromanceinc.com.
3. Ibid. Fiore, "*The Five Kinds of Guys Who Use Online Dating,*" Online Allure Module 2, Lesson 1, accessed April 24, 2018, https://digitalromance.com.
4. Ibid.
5. Dating Sites Reviews, accessed August 21, 2018, https://datingsitesreviews.com.
6. Ibid.
7. Wikipedia Dictionary, s.v. "text messaging," accessed August 21, 2018, https://en.wikipedia.org/wiki/.
8. Ibid. s.v. "e-mail".

9. Ibid. s.v. "instant text message".
10. Ibid. s.v. "online chat"
11. Ibid.

Chapter Ten

1. Ibid. Fiore.
2. Ibid.
3. Ibid.
4. Ibid.
5. Ibid.
6. Zoosk.com. *"Zoosk's First Study of Romance in 2018,"* accessed August, 24, 2018, https://www.datingsitesreviews. com/article.php?story=zoosk-s-first-study-of-the-year-reveals-the-state-of-romance-in-2018, Feb. 13, 2018.

Chapter Eleven

1. FBI.com, accessed August 21, 2018, https://www.fbi.com.
2. Wymoo Investigators, *"Romania Romance Scams Increase, Say Romania Private Investigators,"* accessed August 21, 2018. https://www.wymoo.com/contact-us, 2016.
3. Ibid. FBI.
4. McGraw, Phil Dr., Television Show, accessed September 10, 2018, https://www.drphil.com/shows/two-sisters-confront-their-mom-who-says-shes-married-to-tyler-perry-can-karla-be-convinced-she-was-scammed, July 26, 2018.

Chapter Fourteen

1. Movie, "Letter to Juliet," accessed August 21, 2018.
2. What, s.v. "what", accessed October 28, 2018, https://en.oxforddictionaries.com/definition/what.
3. If, s.v. "if," accessed October 28, 2018, https://www.dictionary. com/browse/if?s=t.
4. Robert Frost, "The Road Not Taken," *Mountain Interval, (New York: Holt), 1916.*

BIBLIOGRAPHY

Alexis, Sabrina. *"11 Undeniable Signs He's in Love with You."* A New Mode. Accessed October 31, 2018. https://www.anewmode.com/dating-relationships/signs-he-is-in-love-with-you/. 2018.

Cavallo, Carlos. Audio: *"Understanding Men."* Accessed May 1, 2018. https.//www.dating+adviceguru.com.

Dating Sites Reviews. Accessed September 20, 2018. https://datingsitesreviews.com.

Dictionary.com. s.v. "what." Accessed October 28, 2018. http://www.dictionary.com/browse/grief.

Dictionary.com. s.v. "if". Accessed October 28, 2018. http://www.dictionary.com/browse/grief.

DiDonato, Theresa E. Ph.D. Psychologytoday.com. Accessed October 31, 2018. https://www.psychologytoday.com/us/experts/theresa-e-didonato-phd. 2018.

eHarmony.com. *"Dealing with Objections to your New Relationship from your Adult Children."* Accessed August 1, 2018. http://eharmony.com./datingadvice.

Einstein, Albert. *Brainyquote.com.* Accessed June 1, 2018. https://www.brainyquote.com/quotes/albert_einstein_121993.

FBI. Accessed June 20, 2018. https://www.fbi.com.

Fiore, Michael. *"The Magnetic Online Dating Mindset,"* Online Allure, Module 1, Lesson 2, http://digitalromanceinc.com. 2013.

Fiore, Michael. *"Online Dating Heaven, Online Dating Hell."* Online Allure: Module 1. Lesson 2. Accessed July 21, 2018. http://digitalromanceinc.com. 2013.

Fiore, Michael. *"The Five Kinds of Guys Who Use Online Dating,"* Online Allure Module 2, Lesson 1. Accessed April 24, 2018. https://digitalromance.com.

Fiore, Michael. *"The Truth About Online Dating."* Online Allure: Module 1. Lesson 1. Accessed July 21, 2018. http://digitalromanceinc.com. 2013.

Frost, Robert. *Mountain Interval.* (New York: Holt). 1916.

Greene, Vivian. *Goodreads Inc.* Accessed August 21, 2018. https://www.goodreads.com/quotes/132836-life-isn-t-about-waiting-for-the-storm-to-pass-it-s-about.

Harvey, Steve. *Act Like a Lady, Think Like a Man.* (New York: Harper-Collins). 2009.

Kinrys, Marni. *That's Not How Men Work.* (Venice, CA, 2017). www.thatsnothowmenwork.com. P. 65-79.

McGraw, Phil Dr. "Dr. Phil Show." July 26, 2018. Accessed September 10, 2018. https://www.drphil.com/shows/two-sisters-confront-their-mom-who-says-shes-married-to-tyler-perry-can-karla-be-convinced-she-was-scammed. 2018.

Movie. Letter to Juliet. Accessed August 21, 2018.

Oxford Living Dictionaries. s.v. "attraction." Accessed August 20, 2018. https://en.oxforddictionaries.com/definition/attraction.

Oxford Living Dictionaries. s.v. "love." Accessed August 20, 2018. https://en.oxforddictionaries.com/definition/love.

Oxford Living Dictionaries. s.v. "lust." Accessed August 20, 2018. https://en.oxforddictionaries.com/definition/lust.

Pascal, Blaise. *"7 Stages of Grief."* Journey Through Grief. Accessed August 20, 2018. http://www.journey-through-grief.com/7-stages-of-grief.html.

Pope, Bella. *"Does She Love Me? 15 Signs She Actually Loves You."* Accessed October 31, 2018. https://www.everydayknow.com/does-she-love-me/. 2017.

Regurgitate. s.v. "regurgitate". Accessed October 31, 2018. https://en.oxforddictionaries.com/definition/regurgitate.

Ryan, Kevin. *The Business Insider.* Accessed August 21, 2018. (New York). 2009.

The Holy Bible. KJV. Genesis 1:1.

The Holy Bible. KJV. Genesis 1:27.

The Holy Bible. KJV. Genesis 1:31.

The Holy Bible. KJV. Genesis 2:24 and Ephesians 5:31.

The Holy Bible. NIV. I Corinthians 13:4-7.

The Holy Bible. NJV. Revelation 21:4.

The Holy Bible. KJV. Revelation 24.4.

Vocabulary.com. s.v. "attract." Accessed, September18, 2018. https:/www.vocabulary.com/dictionary/attract.

Wikipedia Dictionary. s.v. "text messaging." Accessed August 21, 2018. https://en.wikipedia.org/wiki/.

Wikipedia Dictionary. s.v. "e-mail." Accessed August 21, 2018. https://en.wikipedia.org/wiki/.

Wikipedia Dictionary. s.v. "instant text message." Accessed August 21, 2018. https://en.wikipedia.org/wiki/.

Wikipedia Dictionary. s.v. "online chat." Accessed August 21, 2018. https://en.wikipedia.org/wiki/.

WebMD.com. "*Understanding Sexually Transmitted Diseases (STDs)*." Accessed August 19, 2018. http://www.webMD. com. 2017.

Wymoo Investigators. "*Romania Romance Scams Increase, Say Romania Private Investigators*." Accessed July 19, 2018. https://www.wymoo.com/contact-us. 2016.

Zoosk. "*Zoosk's First Study of Romance in 2018.* Datingsitereviews.com. Accessed April 24, 2018. https://datingsitesreviews.com. 2018.

ABOUT THE AUTHOR

Shelby Wagner was born in an old-fashioned country home in northeast Arkansas, the same house in which her mother had been born. She was raised in a loving Christian home with two siblings. Her family moved to Michigan when she was nine. She started piano lessons when she was twelve and became church organist at sixteen. She is the mother of two children, and has one grandson. She is a retired music teacher, church musician and an entrepreneur.

Shelby is no stranger to grief having lost her husband of fifty years to heart failure in 2016 and her mother six months later. "Learning to Dance in the Rain" is the story of her journey through grief, self-discovery and renewal. Dealing with the loss of someone you love is one of life's most difficult events and Shelby believes her faith in Jesus Christ, her Lord and Savior, has guided her through this most tragic period.

CPSIA information can be obtained
at www.ICGtesting.com
Printed in the USA
FFHW021810080119
50113066-54977FF